VARIEI

MW00679095

ON LANGUAGE AND LITERACY LEARNING

Linda Lonon Blanton

With a Foreword by Shirley Brice Heath

HEINLE & HEINLE PUBLISHERS
I(T)P *An International Thomson Publishing Company*
Boston, Massachusetts 02116 U.S.A.

New York • London • Bonn • Boston • Detroit • Madrid • Melbourne • Mexico City • Paris •
Singapore • Tokyo • Toronto • Washington • Albany, NY • Belmont, CA • Cincinnati, OH

To Mackie and Jordan Blanton, who gave me the support I needed to leave home to learn about language and literacy learning,

and

To John and Marie Randolph, who included me as family, giving me a home away from home,

and

To teachers and students at the Casablanca (Morocco) American School, who gave me gifts of time, insight, and friendship.

The publication of *Varied Voices: On Language and Literacy Learning* was directed by the members of the Newbury House ESL/EFL Publishing Team at Heinle & Heinle:

Erik Gundersen, Editorial Director
Bruno R. Paul, Market Development Director
Mike Burggren, Production Services Coordinator
Stanley J. Galek, Vice President and Publisher/ESL

Also participating in the publication of this program were:

Assistant Editor: Heide Kaldenbach-Montemayor
Manufacturing Coordinator: Mary Beth Hennebury
Cover Designer: Mike Burggren

Heinle & Heinle Publishers
An International Thomson Publishing Company
Boston, Massachusetts 02116 U.S.A.

Manufactured in the United States of America

ISBN: 0-8384-7962-6

10 9 8 7 6 5 4 3 2 1

TABLE OF CONTENTS

FOREWORD

Shirley Brice Heath

Should we have stayed at home and thought of here?
Where should we be today?
Is it right to be watching strangers in a play
In this strangest of theatres?

These lines from Elizabeth Bishop's poem "Questions of Travel" remind us that too often we do stay at home and think only of here. With Blanton's book and her stories of other places, we come to see our own better. Moreover, we come to know that place that most of us as teachers feel we already know too well—classrooms. Blanton takes us in this book into language and literacy learning in settings that appear at first familiar and then strange. The strangeness comes as we recognize just how many views and voices we move through with Blanton. She makes us travel to strange and unexpected literacy events with young children, who seem to expect us to be very comfortable just as they are in their many ways of reading, writing, and working with stories. It is with the eye of the ethnographer that Blanton portrays the stories here. Within a new country, she observed and participated to the extent possible in one of the few sites open to an outside woman in Morocco—a classroom in a school where English was a desired language: the Casablanca American School.

Illustrated in this book are the encircling frames of literacy through which the children of this school in Morocco move. Their views of street signs in scripts and languages announce the influence of multinational corporations and international possibilities of communication as well as the close-up realities of daily shopping, religious life, and forms of work and diversion. Within the school itself, numerous languages come together as background for the English of instruction and activities.

Once we move with Blanton into the classrooms, we have to see the power of multiples of all sorts in the lives of the children—their several languages, numerous homes in other places, and various settings and needs at home for using written English. Three themes stand out in Blanton's book. The first is the blending of oral and written language for the children in whose classrooms she works as ethnographer. These children tell, analyze, illustrate, and dramatize their stories in what seems a natural process of dealing with this strange adult who seems to need so much orientation to early literacy. Next is their juxtaposition of illustration with text—natural companions for making stories in the head and from the eye come alive. The third theme is one that should give heart to language educators who worry that recent advances in our understanding of language acquisition, literate behaviors, and cognitive development have too little influence on teaching and learning in classrooms. The places of study for Blanton were sites that show plenty of influence from recent research findings on how young children develop oral and written language and how they play key social roles in their learning.

This third point is one that Blanton herself illustrates repeatedly, but her work merits further comment than she gives on the issue of roles. By being ethnographer with these children, Blanton enabled them to see her as the uninitiated, the innocent, the naïve. Hence, their knowledge of meta-rules and meta-language comes through again and again. They explain patiently their spelling, classroom duties, journal tasks, and ways of developing meaning. This work demonstrates just how much recent work in the social nature of learning has given us by way of theories. The children with whom Blanton works watch themselves in knowing ways as they become readers and writers, and their awareness of their learning processes becomes evident to us as they act with her as the partner who needs to know more about them and what they are doing. For anyone who has ever doubted that children come to understand phonemic-graphemic correspondences through extensive exposure to print and to drawing meaning from writing and talking stories, this book is a must. These children work in their classrooms so that they become comfortable with themselves as literate learners and with their systems of explanation of just how this learning came about.

Perhaps most important, Blanton's work illustrates a fundamental of the work in cultural anthropology that has led to ethnographies: take a comparative perspective. Blanton's work set against our own knowledge of American classrooms at home allows us to be inside a constant-comparative perspective. We continually have to see ourselves in other settings, have to see the research done in the United States as it is played out in a classroom of multiple languages, cultural backgrounds, and needs. The children of the learning sites studied work as planners moving toward projects to be achieved, goals to be debated together, and an atmosphere of learning to be jointly shaped and multiply-distributed among its members. In what might seem in many ways the "strangest of theatres," the Casablanca American School reassures us of all the ways the research and practices of some of the finest educators elsewhere spread to distant locations and sponsor learning that inspires, illustrates, and tells us again that where we should be today is open to the questions that come with travel.

NOTE TO THE READER

How would I characterize this book? For one, it is a book of stories, stories about others' literacy, language, and learning. It is also a book of stories about my experiences in Morocco and of my learning from others there. It is definitely not a book about me, but I am hoping that my experiences and what I learned from them will interest you. If I succeed in making my experiences real to you—and making sense of them—then I'm hoping you may learn from them, too. More to the point, by sharing them, I hope to set you to thinking about your own experiences in teaching and learning. Then your voice can join the **varied voices** I hope you can hear throughout the book.

For another, it is both a single book, divided into chapters, *and* a compilation of different story essays. What I mean is that I expect you won't read the book from cover to cover, all at once, but may read and work in and out of different chapters at different times. For that reason, I atttempt to build enough information into each chapter, even if redundant about the school setting, so that you won't be lost without having read the preceding chapter(s). I hope this works.

To set up an interactive dynamic, you may want to keep a reader's notebook, or journal, as you read. Note your thoughts, questions, disagreements, stream-of-consciousness ideas—whatever comes to mind. If others are reading the book at the same time, sharing your notes and thoughts with them will enhance the dynamic.

At the end of each chapter, you will find questions and suggestions about aspects of the chapter theme you might want to discuss, reflect on, write about, and research. If you have research plans, you should look ahead to these pages, since some projects take a bit of time.

The book is far from being a solitary effort. In fact, it is as collaborative as the work of the young children I write about. The gifted and dedicated teachers and staff at the Casablanca American School shared their time, good cheer, insights, and classes with me for weeks on end: Melanie Wong Jones, Eileen Achaoui, Marge Gruzen, Patricia Boisseau, Eloise Arnold, Nocha Myers, Ghizlane Benani, Zhor El Ouazzani, Nina Soler, Karima Bencheikh, Karen El Houdigui, Kim Aba, Selwa Harran, Laila Krarssi, Ann Manring, Aimee Meditz, Joan Gally, Anne Osman, and Ana Soler. John Randolph, CAS Director, and Marie Randolph made my work possible. You will hear quite a few of their voices as you read.

The children at the Casablanca American School shared themselves as only children can—unconditionally. There are too many to name, but

I especially want to acknowledge several "big" kids: Raz Raouf and Oumhani Alaoui. Their voices are here too.

Stateside, the voice of Shirley Brice Heath is here, in her own words. But actually it is her voice, as I heard it through her research and writings of the last decade or so, that inspired me to undertake this work. Finally, the wise and reflective voices of five generous colleagues, most of them affiliated with the National Writing Project, can be heard in the questions and suggestions at the end of each chapter, as they put themselves in your shoes as readers of the stories: Troy Vachetta, Carolyn Sanchez, JoEllen Hawkins, Anita Roberts-Long, and Cynthia Roy.

Linda Lonon Blanton

The largest crowds are drawn by the storytellers. It is around them that people throng most densely and stay longest. Their performances are lengthy; an inner ring of listeners squat on the ground and it is some time before they get up. Others, standing, form an outer ring; they, too, hardly move, spellbound by the storyteller's words and gestures. . . The air about the listeners' heads was full of movement, and one who understood as little as I felt great things going on there (p. 77).

Here I am, trying to give an account of something, and as soon as I pause I realize that I have not said anything at all. A marvellously luminous, viscid substance is left behind in me, defying words. Is it the language I did not understand there, and that must now gradually find its translation in me? There were incidents, images, sounds, the meaning of which is only now emerging; that words neither recorded nor edited; that are beyond words, deeper and more equivocal than words (p. 23).

Elias Canetti,
The Voices of Marrakesh

Chapter One

Service Station Attendants and Literacy Acts: Arrival in Morocco

> . . . if we discard childish frames of mind and try to
> grasp the complexity of a situation in which individuals
> act and reflect on their actions, responding to the discon-
> certing demands of the world around them, then what
> seems incoherent becomes intelligible in its existential
> context (p. 12).
>
> —Fatima Mernissi,
> *Beyond the Veil*

RESITUATION

As the airplane banks sharply to the south, the extremes of two continents—Africa and Europe—and two bodies of water—the Atlantic and the Mediterranean—slide silently into view, vividly edged in blues, greens, and browns. I suck in my breath, enraptured. Suddenly I am an astronaut, a giant, a Jack-in-the-Beanstalk, peering down at details of the world far below me. Squinting into the brilliant sunlight, I see the Straits, the Rock, and the densely packed British colony of Gibraltar itself. I can almost make out the cars on Gibraltar's narrow streets.

As the plane rights itself, Tangier, the ancient Moroccan city projecting itself to within a few watery miles of Spain and Gibraltar, slips into view. Then, following the rugged Atlantic coastline, the plane descends rapidly toward Casablanca.

I have traveled this route from Frankfurt to Casablanca a good half-dozen times before this day, but never experienced so powerful a resituating of myself in the world. I am sailing from Europe to the north of Africa, from the West to the *Maghrib*, from a place

1

where I feel relatively anchored—and sure of myself—to one where I feel afloat—and decidedly unsure.

I breathe deeply and struggle to project my thoughts forward, to the weeks that lie ahead. I am coming to Casablanca to study language and literacy, to observe children learning English and becoming readers and writers—all more or less at the same time. The complicated part for the kids is that their literacy will be intertwined in English, the language they are still in the process of learning. I don't doubt that the kids can pull it off, but can I? I have never done ethnographic research before, except in my own classroom; literacy is still a new subject for me, despite the crash course I have given myself in preparing for this project; and I have never worked with kids so young, spending 25 years working mainly with college students. What if I can't make sense of my observations? What if, after a whole year on this project, I have nothing to report to my university, come next fall, to justify the sabbatical leave I've been given?

As the heavy plane lurches and its wheels screech, slide, and finally settle on the pavement, I pull myself away from doubt to the moment at hand. *They still haven't mowed the grass along the runway,* I mutter to myself. It has been at least three years since my last visit to Morocco, but the boxy contours of the airport terminal, appearing in the distance like a mirage, comfort me in their familiarity, like the first glimpse of known land after a long sea voyage.

Passport control, baggage claim, and customs lie between me and the crush of people sure to be jockeying for space to greet arriving passengers. On this day I hope to see a familiar face waiting for me in the crowd. Since the 1987–88 school year spent setting up an English-language program, I have stayed in touch with colleagues at the Casablanca American School—some are now close friends—and I anticipate one of them breaking free from the school day to meet me.

My footsteps echo on the gleaming marble floor as I wind through the corridors to passport control, my brain anticipating the French and Arabic I will need to negotiate the formalities just ahead. I haven't spoken French or my limited Arabic in several years, but the needs of the moment push my mind out of English gear, to my relief.

The airport seems abnormally quiet, I notice as I reach passport control. And it is eerily empty, except for small clusters of military

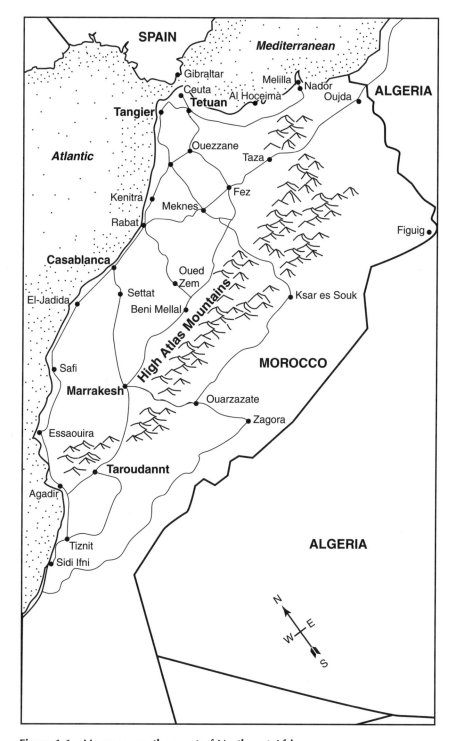

Figure 1-1   Morocco, on the coast of Northwest Africa

police, submachine guns slung over their shoulders. *Odd*, I think—
not remembering such heavy security before.

I inch up to the yellow line at a passport control station and
await my turn. The old man in front of me steps over the line
too soon, arousing disapproving glares from the military police
watching the arriving passengers thread through. Feeling foolish
but nervous about the guns, I check several times to make sure
my feet are *behind* the line and not on it.

When a nod signals my turn, I step forward and hand over my
passport and the arrival card I filled out before landing. Unmoved
by my forced cheerfulness, the passport agent soberly studies the
card, then studies me. Without glancing down, he picks up my
passport, moves it up to his line of vision and examines it, without
loosening his visual lock on me. I feign a calm patience, as my
irritation at his attempts to intimidate me overtakes my ner-
vousness. *No way am I going to act like I have something to hide*, I
mutter to myself.

A burly man, wearing a dark suit, tinted eyeglasses, and a look
of importance, stands at the agent's side. *Is he scrutinizing me or the
agent?* I can't tell. The agent takes forever to process my entry—
another attempt at intimidation?—next loading information about me
into the computer to his side and checking through a long roster
of names. *A list of known terrorists? And he's looking for my name?* Not
finding whatever he's looking for, he waves me through. Despite his
studied gazes, he never once makes eye contact, as if I'm transparent
and he's fixed on an object beyond me.

RECOGNIZING LITERACY

Relieved to have passed muster, I also feel a giddy high that—
among a zillion things going through my mind—I recognize the
passport check as a <u>literacy event.</u> *An odd time for me to be academic*,
I think.

From my readings, I know to think of a literacy event as a basic
unit of observation in literacy research, as an activity involving any
of the following:

a. reading (from decoding letters to reading for comprehension),
b. writing (from copying to creative prose),
c. manipulating written materials or books with the intent to use them
    for some purpose, or

d. behavior or discussion making reference to reading, writing, or other activities in the material culture of literacy (Wagner *et al.*, 1986, 240).

Before leaving for Morocco and my project, I had worried that I might not recognize aspects of literacy new to my conscious awareness, since much of any literate person's engagement in literacy is subconscious, So, standing there in the Casablanca airport, exhausted from my flight, anxious about starting an adventure whose outcome I can't predict, and unsettled by the heavy security and oppressive authority around me, I silently rejoice in recognizing a literacy event. *Reading my passport, "writing" information from the passport into the computer, reading a list for my name. Check (√). Literacy event.*

A second literacy event follows hard on the heels of the first. At this point, I start counting.

Literacy Event #2. I round a corner, arriving at a second passport check. Leafing through my passport, an agent—this one uniformed— inquires about my reason for entering Morocco. To keep things simple, I reply I am there to visit friends at the Casablanca American School. Then, noticing the numerous stamps in my passport, he asks why I've visited Morocco so many times. *Is he thinking I might be a gunrunner? A CIA agent? An international terrorist?* I tell him that I like his country so much, I just keep coming back. Seeming pleased, he scans my handluggage, examines me against my passport photo, and checks the newly entered stamp from passport control. With a smile, he welcomes me to Morocco, and I move on. *Behavior making reference to the material culture of literacy (stamps in my passport). Check (√). Literacy event.*

Literacy Event #3. Finding baggage claim for Lufthansa, I wait for my suitcase. As the carousel turns, producing contents of the flight, baggage handlers, travelers, and airport officials check tags. Half a dozen cartons labeled *Achtung! Ich liebe!* and, in parentheses, *Live birds!* glide past. *Why birds, of all things?* Two young Germans—faces I recognize from the flight—collect the cartons, while a third, with official-looking documents in hand, confers with a uniformed Moroccan. *Manipulating written materials (customs documents) and reading (luggage tags). Check (√). Literacy event.*

As I wait, staring at a now empty carousel, I calculate how to manage without a change of clothes and suppress the mental image of my bag being blown up by explosives experts in Frankfurt, which happens to stray bags at security-conscious German airports

I was told. The carousel is still moving though, which I take as a promise of more bags to come. Finally, coming around the bend, my lone suitcase appears. It is last off the plane.

> **Literacy Event #4.** From baggage claim I move to customs. Again I present my passport. The agent asks why I am in Morocco. Seemingly impressed that I am American—*and I am a teacher*, I add—he places a yellow chalk checkmark on my suitcase, another on my backpack, and waves me on. A bit sheepishly, I move past my fellow travelers, revealing the contents of their lives as they pull everything out of enormous, bulging suitcases and sagging cardboard boxes. Seeing yellow chalk-marks on my bags, the heavily armed policemen at the door leading to the main terminal direct me through. *Behavior making reference to something in the material culture of literacy (chalk marks, meaning "satisfactorily inspected"). Check (√). Literacy event.*

ROADBLOCKS, STREETS ABUZZ

The usual crush of waiting people jostling for space outside customs is nowhere in sight. No familiar face for me. No welcome for anyone. Baffled, I follow other arriving passengers, directed toward an exit to the street.

Once outside, I see the crowd I expected inside, now forced behind security lines in the street. Seeing no one I know, I stand there gazing at them; they gaze back. *What now?* I think. Unable to get to the front of the crowd and too short to peer over, my friend Eileen finally emerges around the edge of the throng and grabs my sleeve. Dragging me to the parking lot, she says she'll explain everything when we get to the car.

Earlier that week, two tourists were killed, shot, in a hotel in Marrakesh, this in a country where murder is rare. In the hunt for the killers, police uncovered a cache of arms in the countryside. Several Algerians carrying French passports have been detained. The airport is under surveillance, tension is high, and security is tight everywhere, Eileen says. The police have erected roadblocks and people on the street are abuzz, but there is little official word in newspapers or on radio and television. Many Moroccans assume that Algerian fundamentalists are attempting to export their revolution to neighboring Morocco, Eileen tells me. *Great,* I think, *I would pick this particular time to come.*

As if to validate Eileen's story, a police roadblock on the road leading into Casablanca appears suddenly, and Eileen slows the car. Seeing how many literacy events I can count during my first hour on the ground in Morocco seems, well, a little silly—given the drama going on around me—but I am committed.

> **Literacy Event #5.** At the roadblock, one policeman greets us, scrutinizes our car from the driver's side, and asks our nationalities. Other armed and uniformed men stand on my side of the car. I hold up my passport. Eileen, a British citizen—or *the Queen's subject*, as she jokingly refers to herself—produces hers, negotiating the formalities in her fluent Arabic. Not quite knowing what to make of us, the policeman on Eileen's side prolongs the check by asking to see her car papers, which she pulls from the glove compartment in a flurry of movement. Ownership papers, driver's license, proof of taxes paid, and who knows what else. Judging by his reaction as he studies each one carefully, the papers are in order. Throughout, Eileen's favorite Elvis tape plays on the cassette deck of the car. *Bless my soul what's wrong with me . . . shaking like a leaf on a tree.* Seeing nothing suspicious, and slightly bemused by the oddity we are, the Moroccan policemen wave us on. *Manipulating written materials (passports and car papers). Check (√). Literacy event.*

Eileen continues her story. A few days earlier, a Royal Air Maroc plane, on a short flight from Agadir to Casablanca, loaded with tourists—including a Kuwaiti prince—crashed moments after takeoff. There were no survivors and little wreckage, since the plane literally flew, nose first, into the ground. The official version is that the pilot committed suicide, taking 45 people with him. No one is buying the official version. An eyewitness claims to have seen the plane explode in midair. Rumors connect the crash to the killings in Marrakesh; speculations are that a bomb was on board, part of the Islamic fundamentalists' *jihad.*

In any case, stories abound of individuals who planned to take a later flight but traded for a ticket on the doomed flight. The story circulates of the off-duty RAM pilot, the first female pilot in Royal Air Maroc's history, who finagled a seat on the flight to join her husband and three-year-old daughter for a weekend in Casablanca. Everyone knows someone who knew someone on the plane.

OUT OF THE STATION, THROUGH THE DOOR

> **Literacy Event #6.** Mid-story, Eileen noses her small Peugeot into a Somepi service station on the outskirts of Casablanca and, in Arabic, asks the attendant for 20 dirhams' worth of fuel, about $2 US. When the

numbers on the pump roll to 20, the attendant removes the nozzle, reattaches it to the pump, and secures the gas cap. Taking the exact change Eileen hands him, he pulls a *facture* from the leather money pouch hanging from a strap on his shoulder, records the date, writes down *Super . . . 20 dh*, and hands Eileen her receipt. Whether literate or not in other aspects of his life, the service station attendant engages with Eileen in a literacy event. *Copying numbers from the gas pump onto a receipt. Check (√). Literacy event.*

Literacy Event #7. From the Somepi station, Eileen and I arrive momentarily at the Casablanca American School. Dashing to get back to class before the final bell, Eileen leaves me with Hamadi, the daytime *gardien*. Although Hamadi seems to recognize me and we exchange brief greetings, he isn't about to let my vague familiarity deter him from following his set procedure for allowing visitors through the gate. Hamadi hands me a clipboard and instructs me to write my name and business at the school. With my name on his clipboard, he slowly decodes the letters. *B-l-an, B-lan.* About half-way through, he looks up from his clipboard and at me. *Blan-ton, Blan-ton.* Now he remembers. *Mais oui, Madame Blanton . . . marhabebik, marhabebik* (welcome) . . . *comment va Monsieur Blanton? Et la petite, comment-va-t-elle?* And on he goes. *Decoding my name. Check (√). Literacy event.*

I am through the door, so to speak, my arrival preceding by moments the end of the school day. As I stand there, engaged in now-extended greetings with Hamadi, little bodies swirl around me, some tugging on my skirt, others rushing past to greet familiar faces arriving to take them home.

Words of the Nobel prize-winning writer Elias Canetti, no ordinary visitor to Morocco, come to mind as expressive of the moment: *th[is] is only the beginning of a complicated affair regarding the outcome of which nothing is known in advance* (p. 21). Canetti is talking about bargaining in the *souks;* I am setting out to learn about language and literacy in these children's classrooms. I desperately hope that, unlike the first price named in the bargaining, the subject of my interest is not an *unfathomable riddle* (p. 21).

◆ REFERENCES

Canetti, E. (1978). *The voices of Marrakesh: A record of a visit.* New York: Farrar Straus Giroux.

Mernissi, F. (1987). *Beyond the veil: Male–female dynamics in modern Muslim society.* Bloomington: Indiana University Press.

Wagner, D. A., Messick, B. M., & Spratt, J. (1986). Studying literacy in Morocco. In B. Schieffelin & P. Gilmore (Eds.), *The acquisition of literacy: Ethnographic perspectives* (pp. 233–260). Norwood, NJ: Ablex.

◆ THOUGHT STARTERS
for reflection, journal writing, and/or discussion:

1. The chapter describes several "literacy events." From what you've read, create your own definition of a literacy event and apply the definition to a day in your own life. What literacy events do you come up with?

2. Think back over your own literacies. Have they changed with age? With circumstance? Explain and illustrate.

3. How is literacy cross-cultural? Do different cultures privilege some literacies over others? Explain. What experiences of yours relate to this?

4. Have you ever been in a situation where no one else spoke your language(s)? Or a situation that could only be mediated through literacy? What happened? How did you feel? What did it take to handle the situation or "deliver" you from it?

◆ PROJECT STARTERS
for writing and research:

1. Keep a journal for five days, noting the literacy events in your life. Take one of the events, describe it in detail, and analyze the process and/or literacy "requirements" you needed to negotiate the event.

2. Write your own literacy autobiography. Any seminal experiences? How/when did you become a writer and reader? What role does literacy play in your life? Any future goals related to literacy? (In a class, sharing autobiographies is a great way for everyone to get acquainted.)

3. View a (short) foreign film without subtitles. Try writing up a summary of the plot. What do you learn about language and literacy from this experience?

Chapter Two

Unruly Experience: How and Why Ethnography?

If ethnography produces cultural interpretations through intense research experience, how is such unruly experience transformed into an authoritative written account? How, precisely, is a garrulous, overdetermined cross-cultural encounter, shot through with power relations and personal cross purposes circumscribed as an adequate version of a more-or-less discrete "other-world," composed by an individual author (quoted in Van Maanen, p. 1)?

—James Clifford,
On Ethnographic Authority

HOW INDEED?

How *is* unruly experience transformed into an authoritative written account? And how, precisely, *is* an overdetermined cross-cultural encounter, shot through with personal cross-purposes, composed by an individual author? How, indeed? Before leaving for Morocco though, I was too busy arranging my life, the going-away part and the being-gone part, to wrestle with these questions.

I cleared the way with the director of the Casablanca American School (CAS), to make sure my intentions were clear and my presence there wouldn't be disruptive. When an official invitation to do my study at CAS arrived, I incorporated it into a lengthy sabbatical leave proposal and then waited for six months for its approval up the administrative line.

Although a full-year sabbatical leave seemed like a luxury and approval of it a university favor, I doubted the wisdom of my request, once it came through. In financial terms, it meant dropping to half-pay, when a full check barely stretched from payday to payday. So I scrambled for extra university funds to cover at least airfare for the two extended trips to Morocco I planned.

It was, in some ways, easier and yet more difficult that my husband and teenage daughter would stay at home, sticking to their routine while I gallivanted half-way around the world. There was no need to shut down a house or find a renter; no utility or charge card accounts to settle and close. But would my husband and daughter be all right without me? Would they eat healthy? Would they eat at all? Would the bills get paid on time? Would my daughter, who would be a senior in high school, manage to navigate the college application process with only one parent at home?

Would I be all right without them? Being of the generation of females too late to be satisfied with domesticity but too early for social revolution, I alternated between guilt and exhilaration at the thought of going off *on my own*. Would my time away amount to abandonment of my family? What sane wife and mother would do as I planned?

Afterwards, when my daughter was admitted to the college of her choice, when no collection agencies telephoned about overdue accounts, when my husband hadn't filed for divorce, Clifford's questions grabbed my full attention. They then became powerful dragons to slay. After all, how could I claim that the views I formulated during my Morocco experience were "true" ones? How could I expect others to accept my experience as valid—and worthy of telling? How would I myself decide what to tell and what to leave out of experience shared daily with others? And finally, how could I translate that daily and ordinary, yet extraordinary, experience into writing that neither trivialized nor formalized it?

THE NATURE OF ETHNOGRAPHY

These are an ethnographer's questions. And they are ultimately inevitable, I finally decided, because of the very nature of ethnography. They stem from understanding what ethnography is.

Above all, ethnography is a study of lived experience. Traditionally, ethnography "belonged" to anthropologists such as Margaret Mead, living among the people of Samoa and studying their cultural practices. It belongs to anthropological linguists like Shirley Brice Heath (1983), studying three communities in the Piedmont region of the southeastern United States to learn about language use in its full-blown and complex context of daily life.

As classroom teachers question quantitative methodologies and what we learn from them, ethnography and case studies have become part of educational research. Think of Glenda Bissex's (1980) study of her son's efforts to become a reader and writer, Anne Haas Dyson's (1981) study of kindergarten children, Chiseri-Strater's (1991) research into the writing of four university students, or Spack's (1997) long-term investigation into the American college learning and writing of a young woman from China. As part of this development, teachers are now ethnographic researchers in their own classrooms with their own students.

Whether as part of educational research or not, ethnographies are, by necessity, *homemade* (Geertz's term, 1988, 145). That is, they are constructed by the ethnographer. My shared experience in Morocco, as told by me, is *my* interpretation, *my* version of reality, yielding a particular knowledge through *my* eyes. And through my eyes, I cannot but encode my own lived experience as student, teacher, traveler, wife, mother, daughter, and female in the world.

From Geertz (1988), I know that my credibility, as ethnographer, comes from my ability to capture the everyday scenes of my experience—its drama and, conversely, its ordinariness. My job is to depict to readers a vivid sense of having been there, so that they can *be there* too. An ethnographer's credibility, in fact, turns on readers' access to the experience.

The focus in ethnography then is not on the ethnographer, the writer of the account, but on the rich, social and cultural context from which the writing arises. As ethnographers study human behavior, they situate their interpretations within that context, in settings that naturally occur (Watson–Gegeo, 1988). My job, as a writer of ethnography, is to make people in their settings come alive for the reader, as I describe what goes on, explain outcomes, and translate, as best I can, what their actions mean to them (p. 576).

What ethnography does for me, as a researcher of language and literacy, is to decrease the distance between me and the subjects of my study. It allows me to access language and literacy as lived experience. Approached ethnographically, language and literacy become part of a daily rhythm, part of how the individuals in my study conduct their lives. Ethnography enables me to participate in their lives and document how seamlessly the children, who I am most interested in, integrate language and literacy into their work and play, and how wise and caring adults guide them in doing so.

If I had had more time and energy to follow the children home from school, ethnography would have also enabled me to avoid the artificial separation between school and home. While I focused primarily on the children's lives at school, ethnography would have allowed me to see more deeply how these kids live language and literacy away from the school setting.

WHY CHOOSE ETHNOGRAPHY?

Why did I choose ethnography for my Morocco study? As much for what it is not, as for what it is. I had no hypotheses I wanted to test. I had long grown weary of quantitative methodologies, finding them unable to capture the universality, yet the distinctiveness, of people and communities, that lies at the heart of everything that interests me. I wanted the *social*, without the *science*. I wanted to be a participant, not simply an observer. I didn't want to conduct an experiment; I wanted to be part of an experience. I wanted to relate to people I already knew and those I would soon know as subjects, not as objects. I did not want to think in terms of correlations or variables. I do not like or know how to use statistics. And I needed a way of proceeding that would allow me to learn about literacy and language without needing to pretend I was an expert.

Actually, it was Andrea Fishman who convinced me to choose ethnography. Before then, though, my question was <u>not</u> *Why ethnography?* but *Why do I think* I *can do ethnography?* Numerous times I had mentally marshaled my forces, lining up a list of answers. I had a Ph.D. in sociolinguistics. While a doctoral student, I had done research in the Appalachian Mountains of Kentucky, navigating my way through a small, close-knit community. I had spent 25 years in the classroom teaching second-language students of English, developing what seemed like an ability to participate with and, at the same time, observe my students learning. I had managed, to my satisfaction, to make sense of their efforts and mine, and to write about and publish my observations. I had lived in North Africa—two years as a Peace Corps volunteer in Tunisia years ago and, more recently, a year in Morocco on a contract with the Casablanca American School, while my husband spent a Fulbright year at the university in Casablanca. So I was neither a stranger to the culture nor to the experience of daily life there. Still I had my doubts.

It was Shirley Heath who introduced me to Andrea Fishman, so to speak. In a conversation about Morocco, I said to Shirley, embarrassed though I was to say it, that I kept wondering why I thought I could do ethnography. *Read Andrea Fishman, she said, and you'll understand not only why you can do ethnography, but why you should.*

As Shirley said, I read and understood. Fishman's concerns were mine, as well as her reasons for choosing how to go about her study. Fishman's (1988) ethnographic study of literacy in a small Amish community, and in the lives of one Amish family, makes for a compelling story about literacy, schooling, human life, and, above all, about how we see ourselves differently if we succeed in looking through the eyes of others. I came away hoping for even a fraction of the power of Fishman's experience and praying for a modicum of her success in sharing it with others. Despite my trepidation, I was hooked—and sure of what I wanted.

As I conducted my research, I began to realize how profoundly ethnography is not just a methodology. More than anything, it is a way of knowing, a way of being in relationship to others. It assumes that I, as ethnographer, and my thinking are validated in the validity of others' thoughts. That my views are authenticated by the authenticity of others' views. And that I construct my meaning through the connections with those around me. Choosing ethnography ultimately says something about our perceptions of the nature of knowledge, about how we know.

ETHNOGRAPHIC TOOLS, ETHNOGRAPHIC LIFE

What were my ethnographic "tools"? Simply, a video camera, a notebook, a tape recorder, and my eyes and ears. And here is what I did with them. I observed classes. I played with kids and watched them play. I read to kids, and I listened to them read to me, to their teachers, and to each other. I videotaped kids learning, often seeing a magnified eyeball appear at the other end of my camera lens. (Giggles inevitably ensued.) I videotaped teachers teaching. I took notes and scribbled ideas, and then sometimes got so absorbed in what was going on around me that I forgot to write anything down. I talked to teachers and staff and listened as they talked to me about their concerns and their teaching. And sometimes the best things happened when I had packed up my gear and thought I was through for the day.

I attended birthday parties, sports rallies, and musical programs. I rode the old blue school bus on field trips. I talked to parents and listened to them talking to each other about their kids. I took weekend trips into the countryside by myself and with friends. As a guest, I ate meals in homes and in restaurants. I looked up people I knew from my old neighborhood in Casablanca and walked around the city. I spent time in the homes of Moroccans, Europeans, and Americans.

The thing about ethnography is that once you start, you don't stop. As you participate, you observe. Sometimes you record your observation, sometimes you don't. Absent a notepad in hand, you make a mental note, or simply absorb life swirling around you. With ethnography, there is no 9:00 to 5:00.

By looking back at my datebook, I can reconstruct the schedule of a not-unordinary day:

September 16, 1994

9:00   Talk to Aimee [coordinator of ESL] about ESL team-teaching for kinder and pre-first. How is it working out?

9:40-11:00   Videotape Eileen's pull-out ESL class [first graders].

11:30   Lunch with Meriam [a friend and mother of one CAS graduate and two current CAS students], her house.

1:00   Observe Ann's 3rd graders tutor Melanie's kinder class.

2:00   Catch Marge [pre-first teacher] during free period; tape-record her talking about language and literacy.

3:00   Interview Oum-hani [a 12th grader] about her writing.

4:00   Go home with Eileen. [Eileen makes tea, while I play with Ghizlane, her five-year-old. Ghizlane asks me to read Is Your Mama a Lama?, *my gift to her from the States. After reading it to her, I ask her to read it to me. She can't read in English, she claims, but proceeds, turning each page slowly and, in deliberate intonation, pretend-reads what she calls "Little Baby Bambi." Then, at her invitation, I tape-record her reading it again. Each time she ends with "They live happily forever." Enthralled by the tape recorder, Ghizlane asks me to tape her reading the story in Arabic. Same deliberate intonation and turning of pages. Ghizlane wants me to also tape her reading her little* cahier *from French nursery school. Eileen protests, but I am as enthralled by Ghizlane as she is by the recorder.]*

6:00 To the hammam *[public bath] with Eileen. [I forget my differentness as the women, none of whom I know and some of whom enter veiled into the outer room of this public-private space, make room for my clothes on a long bench. An attendant gives me a dollop of black, oily soap tucked into a cone of torn newspaper page and directs me to a scrubber, a woman who, with a loofa, rubs my skin several layers deep to an earlier softness. In the dark, steamy otherworld of the* hammam, *lying on warm marble and enveloped by the soft chatter and gentle laughter from female bodies, I am both a participant and an observer.]*

This is how you do ethnography. The whys are more complex. While related primarily to the reasons discussed in the chapter, the whys are also connected to a desire to diminish the distance between personal life and professional work—to examine one in light of the other, in order to illuminate both.

◆ REFERENCES

Bissex, G. L. (1980). *GNYS AT WRK: A child learns to read and write.* Cambridge, MA: Harvard UP.

Chiseri–Strater, E. (1991). *Academic literacies: The public and private discourse of university students.* Portsmouth, NH: Boynton/Cook Heinemann.

Clifford, J. (1983). On ethnographic authority. *Representations* 1: 118–46.

Dyson, A. H. (1981). *A case study examination of the role of oral language in writing processes of kindergarteners.* Unpublished doctoral dissertation, The University of Texas at Austin.

Fishman, A. (1988). *Amish literacy: What and how it means.* Portsmouth, NH: Heinemann.

Geertz, C. (1988). *Works and lives: The anthropologist as author.* Stanford: Stanford UP.

Hammersley, M. (1990). *Reading ethnographic research: A critical guide.* London: Longman.

Heath, S. B. (1983). *Ways with words: Language, life, and work in communities and classrooms.* New York: Cambridge UP.

Spack, R. (1997). The acquisition of academic literacy in a second language: A longitudinal case study. *Written Communication, 14*(1), 3–62.

Van Maanen, J. (1988). *Tales of the field: On writing ethnography.* Chicago: University of Chicago Press.

Watson–Gegeo, K. A. (1988). Ethnography in ESL: Defining the essentials. *TESOL Quarterly, 22,* 575–592.

◆ RELATED REFERENCES

Heath, S. B. (1982). Ethnography in education: Defining the essentials. In P. Gilmore & A. A. Glatthorn (Eds.), *Children in and out of school: Ethnography and education* (pp. 33–55). Washington, DC: Center for Applied Linguistics.

Hornberger, N. H. (1994). Ethnography. In A. Cumming (Ed.), Alternatives in TESOL Research: Descriptive, interpretive, and ideological orientations (pp. 688–690). *TESOL Quarterly, 28*(4), 673–703.

Leki, I. (1995). Coping strategies of ESL students in writing tasks across the disciplines. *TESOL Quarterly, 29,* 235–260.

◆ THOUGHT STARTERS
for reflection, journal writing, and/or discussion:

1. By its nature, ethnography attempts to explain complex behaviors and processes. Why do you think this methodology should not include quantitative measures? Or do you think some quantitative measures are necessary?

2. What experiences in your life could best be "rendered" ethnographically? Explain. Choose one to tell about.

3. If you had a chance to spend a year as an ethnographic researcher, what would you study? Why?

4. If you recorded an ordinary day in a class you were taking or teaching, what kind of thing would you choose to record? What would be the possible benefits?

◆ PROJECT STARTERS
for writing and research:

1. Writing ethnographically, describe the culture in which your literacy has developed. Is it diverse? Academically oriented? (You might want to share your writing.)

2. The style used by ethnographers is highly personal. Two researchers studying the same phenomenon may select very different events to emphasize in their written accounts. Select two ethnographic journal

articles on the same topic and compare both the styles and findings of the researchers.

3. Review Fishman's (1988) study of an Amish family. Describe her "ethnographic tools" and "ethnographic life." Or take Heath's *Ways with Words* (1983).

4. A personal journal can be used for ethnographic research. Over the week, spend 15 or so minutes a day thinking about and noting aspects of your daily life. At the end of the week, write up your notes. (Share your writing if you don't mind.)

Chapter Three

Views of Morocco: Context for a Culturally and Linguistically Diverse School

It was afternoon in the busy Ben Sliman quarter of Casablanca. Crates of fresh vegetables and fruit spilled from shops onto the sidewalk on Rue Lafayette below. Cars and motorbikes rattled by in the streets in a constant rush. It seemed that all the young men sitting in the cafe on the corner wore short sleeves and chain-smoked cigarettes, though now and then an older man in a dark burnous or djellaba hobbled past, like a monk or someone out of the Middle Ages. Women hurried by in high, spiked heels, crossing the street in front of barefoot peddlers driving carts pulled by donkeys (p. 81).

—Tony Ardizzone,
Larabi's Ox

STRIKING JUXTAPOSITION

The Casablanca American School, in its physical presence in Morocco, contradicts the senses, as much as spiked-heeled women hurrying past barefoot peddlers and *djellabaed* old men. Situated since 1990 in a gleaming white, space-age structure, built in what was then a pasture, ten kilometers from the downtown center, the school impresses itself on a landscape that visibly asserts its origins. Scrawny cattle and sheep, herded by ragged boys and turbaned men, still graze on stubby grass beyond the kempt soccer field. Garbage collects in untended areas near the circular school entrance, as city services lag behind the population growth in this northeastern sector of Casablanca, long known, oddly enough, as *Californie*.

Beside the walled playground, donkey carts rattle along the

roadway, dodging late model BMW sedans and Toyota 4Runners ferrying students to and from the school. Behind the school and up the hill, donkey drivers outdistance crazily laden Bedford or Erliet trucks, belching clouds of diesel smoke as they labor to market in Rabat, 50 kilometers to the north. Down the hill, a shantytown of cardboard and corrugated tin shacks hovers over garbage-strewn dirt alleyways.

All the while, sumptuous villas, solid and luminous, spring up around the school, attaching themselves to a modernity perceived as *American*. Some occupants of these grand houses are families of students at the school. Others, attracted by the growing trendiness of the neighborhood and rapidly appreciating land values, are not.

Overall, the transformation of the landscape along the *Route de la Mecque* has been swift. In the summer of 1988, when we picnicked in the pasture that would become the new school grounds, one lone villa, that of the family donating the land for the school, was within sight. Almost a decade later, little of the land lies open and unoccupied.

MOROCCAN SCENES

Whether striking in their contradiction—of poverty and wealth, beauty and squalor, or modernity and medievalism—or simply striking, scenes of Morocco stretch before me, providing a backdrop for the American School:

◇◇◇ Two women share a compartment with me on the train to Fez, the most ancient of imperial Moroccan cities—dating from the ninth century. One wears a long, dark caftan, her head enveloped in a headscarf pleated around her barely visible face. Intricate designs, etched in ocher-red henna, encircle her hands and sandaled feet. The other woman, also Moroccan, wears a modish drop-waist dress, paisley blue-green in pattern, with black, lace-up ankle boots and green cotton socks, the tops casually bunched at the ankle. A Sony Walkman holds down her headful of springy curls. At her side, cassette cases reveal her choice of music—Pink Floyd, James Lee Hooker, Tracy Chapman.

◇◇◇ From the window, as the train stops at Ben Slimane, on this same trip to Fez, I watch a young mother, caftaned and veiled, holding the hands of two young boys. The boys are wearing Dallas Cowboy baseball caps—turned backwards—baggy faded jeans, and high-top Nikes. Motionless, the three watch the arrival of the train.

◇◇◇ In the Maarif, an area in central Casablanca closed to Moroccans during the French Protectorate in the first half of this century but now home to mostly a Moroccan population, flower stalls of long-stemmed red, yellow, and pink roses line the street next to the central market. Inside the stuccoed walls of the market, pungent smells rise from enormous baskets of spices, the loose spices patted into tall, gravity-defying cones—deep red paprika, yellow saffron, dusty green tarragon. Several stalls down, slabs of horse meat, sheep entrails, and freshly plucked chickens, heads and feet attached, dangle from hooks. Nearby, mountains of bright orange nectarines, plump, red strawberries, and yellow apples compete in vividness with vats of black, wrinkled olives and mounds of shiny green peppers, outdone only by purple eggplants, the size of footballs, fist-sized, red tomatoes, and bushy, green bouquets of cilantro.

◇◇◇ One afternoon, I am in the Maarif, at the stall of a flower vendor who usually bargains fairly with me, watching while a young, Western-dressed Moroccan haggles over the price of roses. As consensus eludes them, the volume of their voices rises. Insulted, the vendor refuses to lower the price to what the shopper wants to pay, which, judging by the late-model car she has driven to the market, he deems unfair. She accuses him of thinking her stupid enough to pay a foreigner's price. Neither budges, and she huffs off to her BMW, hurling insults as she goes. Shrugging his shoulders and telling no one in particular he'd rather keep his roses than sell to her, he turns to wait on me and, without much resistance, gives me an extra-good price on this day. Though all aspects of life in Morocco involve negotiation, the flower scene is notable only in that such transactions usually take place quickly and quietly, rarely becoming contentious.

◇◇◇ On the flat roofs of the tightly packed Maarif, amid the clotheslines draped with fluttering clothes and blankets hauled out for airing, satellite dishes sprout like mushrooms. Now that the government has lifted the ban on foreign transmissions, German soap operas, Spanish soccer matches, French movies, American talk shows (*Oprah!*) fill the airwaves.

◇◇◇ Three illuminated signs, unusual in their juxtaposition only to a Westerner, greet passengers crossing the cavernous Rabat train station. One gives directions to the *toilettes;* another, to the *chef de gare,* the official in charge; and the third, to the *salle de prière* (prayer room).

◇◇◇ A cafe, bordering the Atlantic in the Ain Diab section of Casablanca, fills with men, their *mopeds* (motorized bicycles) parked in rows nearby. Some in *djellabas*, others in jeans, chain-smoke cigarettes and drink small glasses of sugary, steaming mint tea. Along the *corniche*, past the Lido and Kon Tiki beach clubs, at a new McDonald's—its golden arches projecting high—late model Fiats, Audis, and Jeep

Figure 3-1   Striking juxtaposition of open-air market stalls and nearby modern mall shopping

Cherokees queue up to order Big Macs and Happy Meals at the drive-through window. Directed by a traffic policeman, other drivers flow into the lot to park, eat inside, and let their children play on the shiny, multicolored jungle gym, supervised by Ronald McDonald.

◇◇◇ I wander through the narrow, labyrinthine passageways of the Fez *medina*, shafts of dusty light breaking through the overhead transoms. The smells threaten to overwhelm me—excrement, sandlewood, olive oil, saffron, newly cured leather. Hearing a mule driver's cries of *balek! balek!* (watch out!), I spring to the side, pressing against a wall to let the beast pass. Tied to the back of the mule is a Sony television set, swaying perilously, as the hooves of the mule slip and slide on the worn cobblestones. With my guides, two American Peace Corps volunteers living in Fez, I enter an ancient *fondouk* (inn). Its carved, cedarwood balconies ring the upper floors around a central courtyard, where travelers in the fourteenth century stabled horses and donkeys for the night before ascending to their rooms—bachelors on the second floor, married couples above. Passing the pottery *souks*—brilliant blue, green, and yellow hand-painted bowls crowding their walls—we reach the shop of Laila and Jennifer's friend Muhammad, who has invited us to drink mint tea and see his antique Berber rugs newly arrived from the High Atlas.

◇◇◇ In the estimation of students in her English classes at *Université Sidi Mohamed Ben Abdellah* in Fez, Laila simply cannot *be* American. After all, her name is Arabic (meaning "night"). She speaks Arabic, having mastered the native language of her parents as her second language. Being of Middle Eastern descent, she looks Arab and, therefore, Moroccan. And, holding on to the religious faith of her family, she is a Muslim. Deciding to end the debate, Laila takes her American passport to class to demonstrate to her students her citizenship. Examining it, one student exclaims *Aha! They* are *right. She* isn't *American!* He has noted that her birthplace is Alexandria, Egypt. (Her family immigrated to the United States when she was two years old.) Laila throws up her hands, resigned to their thinking what they will.

◇◇◇ At Moroccan school examination time, students walk alone in public gardens or pace under street lights at night, notebook in hand, quietly reciting their class lessons, a practice reflective of Islamic instruction, whose goal is to memorize the Quran.

◇◇◇ Whether gazing at the horizon in the valley of the Drâa—in the arid south of Morocco—beyond dark shafts of rock and mud-clay, crenelated, and towered walls of a *ksar*, or looking across the ever-crowded *Parc de la Ligue Arabe* in Casablanca, you are struck by the quality of the light—intense, luminous, brilliant—every detail magnified, as if viewed through newly prescribed lenses. So it is with the quality of the sound:

[Y]ou notice the stillness. An incredible, absolute silence prevails outside the towns; and within, even in busy places like the markets, there is a hushed quality in the air, as if the quiet were a constant force which, resenting the intrusion of sound, minimizes and disperses it straightaway (Bowles, 1993).

Luminous light and hushed quiet.

CASABLANCA

Casablanca, *Dar el Baida* (literally, "house white"), is the chief city of Morocco, capital in all but administration, which is located in Rabat, 50 kilometers to the north, along the Atlantic coast. Now the largest in the *Maghrib*, the port of Casablanca is busier even than Marseilles, the city upon which Casablanca was modeled by the French (Ellingham & McVeigh, 1985). When the wind is blowing just right, in the warm months of the year, the odor of phosphate pervades the city, as the white powdered mineral, a component of fertilizer and Morocco's chief export, is pumped into the holds of waiting ships.

Not a pretty city, Casablanca has a utilitarian feel, revealing its

Figure 3-2 Casablanca, seen here from a rooftop, has a utilitarian feel.

early-twentieth-century origin as a base for French commercial development. When France established control over Morocco in 1912, Fez was the commercial center; Tangier, its chief port. But with the north of the country in Spanish hands then—both Fez and Tangier being in the north—the French set about, rapidly and deliberately, to develop Casablanca for their own economic purposes.

Although Morocco gained independence in 1956, Casablanca retains the character created for it by the French. It remains the commercial and economic center of Morocco. And, from a town of twenty or so thousand before 1912, Casablanca has become a sprawling metropolis of several million.

Still growing at a rate of 50,000 or so a year, with the population emigrating from the countryside, primarily from the south, Casablanca is a first-generation city (Ellingham & McVeigh, 1985). A city in constant flux, its inhabitants travel to and from their ancestral birthplaces, crowding into buses, trains, and long-distance taxis, loaded with enormous parcels, to celebrate *Aid el Kabir* and other major Muslim holidays.

Corner grocery stores, bakeries, and other small commercial operations sustain some extended families, with brothers and male cousins arriving from distant villages to live in makeshift arrangements in spare storerooms, spending next-to-nothing and plowing meager profits back into the business. Working from dawn to dark, seven days a week, these workers are still luckier than their countrymen squatting in *bidonvilles* on the outskirts of town. Cobbled together of scavenged tin and cardboard, these miserable shantytowns overflow with those who have neither jobs nor relatives to sustain them in Casablanca and no economic prospects to draw them elsewhere.

Inhabiting the same city but a different world, a wealthy elite—often descended from *Fessi* (from imperial Fez) aristocracy—lives sumptuously in walled, bougainvillea-draped villas along the hushed, curved streets of the Anfa *quartier* of Casablanca. Among these grand, old money houses stands the Villa Mirador, the residence of the American Consul General, a room in which Roosevelt, Churchill, and Stalin signed World War II to its end.

Some elites, seeking greater space, are building larger, even grander show homes in *Californie*. Their tony houses, with tended gardens and illuminated swimming pools, match in elegance any featured on the slick pages of *Architectural Digest*. Other elites, said to be Kuwaitis and Saudis, are buying newly constructed, half-

Figure 3-3
This map of Casablanca shows the geographical proximity of some places mentioned in the text.

million dollar, high-rise condominiums, whose brilliant white, stuccoed and marble exteriors dominate tree-lined streets where smaller, more modest French colonial buildings once stood.

A small but growing middle class, made up of functionaries and small entrepreneurs, occupies older, Mediterranean-style apartment blocks in Gautier and the Maarif. Or they live in solid, free-standing houses in Mers Sultan, a genteel neighborhood whose geographical and emotional center is the *habbous*, an area designated by the king for his special protection. In the *habbous*—next to the royal palace, whose stark white walls and dark green shuttered windows bespeak solitude—row after row of artisans, tailors, and silversmiths, sitting in boxlike stalls, sew and etch. The sounds of their industry fill the warm air.

Hanging outside the clothing stalls of the *habbous,* newly stitched caftans lift to catch the afternoon breeze and flag down prospective customers. Outside the silver stalls, brilliantly polished platters and ornate teapots, waiting to be gifted to brides and grooms, catch the glint of the sun's rays, blinding those who would pass without a glance their way.

MULTILINGUAL SOCIETY

At the small grocery store where I shop, Rachid follows me with a basket, collecting the plump tomatoes and shiny peppers I select from the wooden crates lining the sidewalk. Having arrived in Casablanca several years earlier, with little formal schooling, to work for his cousin Brahim, who owns the store, Rachid transacts business with me in French. Then, depositing me and my vegetables with Brahim, to tally up the bill, Rachid shifts into Arabic to help the next customer. Turning to Brahim to inquire about something he can't immediately locate, Rachid speaks in Berber, his family language. Linguistically speaking, this is not an extraordinary Moroccan scene.

Berber and Arabic, the two indigenous languages of Morocco, and French, a colonial legacy, comprise the primary components of the multilingual mix characterizing modern Morocco. While English is wildly popular among young, Western-oriented Moroccans, who crowd into English classes at the Language Center near the American Consulate on Boulevard Moulay Youssef, English is not widely spoken. Spanish, although spoken more widely in the northern extreme of Morocco, is not wildly popular, despite Morocco's close geographical proximity to Spain—visible on a clear day across the Straits of Gibraltar—and even closer proximity to Ceuta, a Spanish colonial remnant on the North African side of the Straits.

Berber (*tamazight*), the language of a people inhabiting the north of Africa long before the Arabs began arriving in the eighth century, is spoken as a native language by about half the population of modern-day Morocco. The other half natively speaks colloquial Arabic (*derija*).

Arabic-speaking Moroccans tend not to become fluent in Berber. Berbers, however, especially Berber men leaving the mountains or southern villages for work, often become fluent in Arabic. Berber, spoken in three different dialectal forms, is not written, nor is colloquial Arabic (Wagner *et al.*, 1986).

The language of literacy in Moroccan schools is standard Arabic, distinguished from classical Arabic as follows:

> 'Standard' and 'classical' Arabic may be considered as two written varieties. The 'classical' variety is that of the ancient, religious, or formal texts, with the Quran as the penultimate example. Usually, 'standard' Arabic is the modern written form taught in schools in Morocco and other Arabic-speaking countries (Wagner *et al.*, p. 235, cited in a footnote and attributed to A. Ezzaki).

Only males trained in traditional Islamic studies—more likely in an earlier time—would have received literacy instruction in classical Arabic. And only in elite or private primary schools would children in contemporary Morocco receive literacy instruction in French. Such is the case of my friend Eileen's young daughter, enrolled in a private school, where she is gaining literacy simultaneously in Arabic *and* French.

Since standard Arabic, the language of literacy in contemporary Moroccan schools, is a different variety of Arabic from *derija* (colloquial/spoken Moroccan Arabic) and is totally unrelated to *tamazight* (Berber), all children in Moroccan public schools, then, first learn to read and write in a language that none of them speaks. It's fair to point out, though, that the language of literacy is "less foreign" to *derija*-speaking children.

So, the multilingual puzzle breaks into four or five pieces, depending how you count—Berber, colloquial Arabic, standard Arabic, classical Arabic, and French—of three different language families—Hamitic, Semitic (the Arabics), and Indo-European. Like Rachid, my helper at the grocery store, Moroccans, educated or not, often shift in and out of Berber, Arabic, and French—or at least Arabic and French—during the course of a day or even a single conversation. Add in acquaintance or even fluency in Spanish and/ or English, and communication in Morocco becomes a real *tchout-chouka* (mixed salad).

LOOKING FOR CAUSES OF LINGUISTIC VERSATILITY

Aside from simple opportunity to acquire multiple languages, what is it about Moroccans, as a people, that makes them so linguistically versatile? Several social traits stand out.

For one, Moroccans are extremely sociable—warm, expressive, tactile, and outgoing. Shaking hands, both when they see you and when they depart your company, they kiss you on both cheeks, sometimes several times, back and forth, back and forth. Making steady eye contact, they smile and engage in extended greetings, translatable as *Good morning, how are you? Fine? Thanks to Allah! How's your husband? He's fine? Thanks to Allah! And your daughter? How is she? Fine? Thanks to Allah! And how are you? You're fine? Thanks to Allah!* Adding silent thanksgiving that you're all right, they touch their hands to their hearts, further extending honor by lightly brushing their lips with their hand after shaking yours.

Noticeable as an aspect of their sociability, Moroccans seem to avoid being alone, living in close quarters even when other arrangements are possible. They tend to congregate in groups, together spending long afternoons in cafes, drinking muddy coffee from tiny cups or mint tea from little colored glasses, walking in public gardens or chatting in public squares. Along the roadway, even in the otherwise deserted countryside, no houses in sight, men in dark *burnouses,* pointed hoods pulled over their heads to ward off the chill, cluster together, squatting on the ground or leaning against a grassy bank to catch the weak rays of a winter sun.

Eternally hospitable, Moroccans eagerly serve guests mint tea and sugery pastries, if not a lamb *tagine* or vegetable *couscous,* topped with almonds and raisins. Once, traveling by donkey in the mountains, my daughter and I and some friends came upon a tiny village, dirt poor, a few scrawny chickens scratching beside square mud dwellings. Several children of the village saw us coming and ran ahead to tell the others. By the time we arrived, the adults were preparing for us. Insistent on serving us tea, and espe-

Figure 3-4 Moroccan men traditionally wear *burnouses*.

cially excited that a child of another culture was among them, they were too sincere in their invitation for us to refuse, despite our self-consciousness at stressing their meager resources.

As we sat on thick, woven rugs in the home selected for us to enter, the master of the house engaged us in the traditional ritual of tea-making. Pushing sprigs of fresh green mint into a round-bellied teapot, then adding lumps of sugar, our host tested the strength of the tea—back and forth, back and forth, from a glass to the pot—until it met his satisfaction. Then holding the pot high and pouring the amber-green liquid in a steaming arc into small colored glasses, he readied the tea for serving to his guests, reserving the first half-glass for himself as the test glass. Picking up the hot glasses at the rim, we sipped the steaming tea, *chai naa-naa* (Arabic) or *thé à la menthe* (French), engaging in the ritual ceremony of tea-drinking. By extending their hospitality, the villagers honored us. By gratefully accepting their hospitality, we honored them.

Surely also a factor in Moroccans' linguistic versatility is their lack of affectation. Genuine and sincere, Moroccans focus on communicating, caring more about the message and the interaction with their interlocutor than about correctness or form. Fascinated by their linguistic and social grace, I never tire of studying Moroccans socializing with both friends and new acquaintances. I study them, I suppose, to learn the secret of their success, hoping to appropriate some of it for myself.

Along with being sociable and unaffected, or perhaps because of it, Moroccans are not linguistic purists. Surely this is also a factor in their linguistic versatility. To them, no one language seems better than any other, and, as far as they are concerned, languages—any languages they know, even partially—can be used and used in combination. Time and again, I've been in conversations that made use of French *and* Arabic *and* English—even heard single sentences interweaving all three languages. Yet the languages retain their own integrity, and I never hear them combined unintelligibly.

MULTILITERATE SOCIETY

Universal education is legally mandated in Morocco, and has been since independence in 1956, when the national school system was established. Education is valued and, unlike the old days when one son in the family might be selected for religious schooling, it is seen today as a right for *all* children. And because the written language of the Quran is considered sacred, education—even modern secular education, with literacy as its by-product—is especially valued. Drive through any Moroccan town at midday during most seasons of the year and you'll see boys and girls, wearing pale blue school smocks, bulky bookbags carried like packs on their little

Figure 3-5 The ritual of tea-making

backs, trudging along the road on their way home to lunch or back
to school.

A red and green Moroccan flag flying from its roof, set back
from the road miles from any town, a rural school may be no more

than a single, concrete-block room, with another small room built alongside to house the schoolmaster. But it is still a school, to which children ride donkeys or walk miles, circumstances more related to my elderly mother's memories of an American childhood than to any of my own generation, yet ordinary in rural contemporary Morocco.

Everywhere in Morocco, there is evidence of literacy, signs of what ethnographers of literacy call the *material culture of literacy,* defined as the products of literacy and physical means associated with literate activities (Wagner *et al.,* 1986, p. 254; Heath, 1980; Szwed, 1981). Even from my second-story bedroom window in the home of my friends the Randolphs, the material culture of literacy is visible.

At the corner of my street is a red, octagonal sign, recognizable anywhere in the world as a stop sign, with the word *qof* written large in Arabic script, facing drivers as they reach the intersection of the busy street. The octagonal sign conveys its message— conveys, in fact, its very *sign-ness*—through two different symbolic systems: graphemically (through script) and iconically (through its conventional formulaic design: its color, shape, and markings). For people like me, who cannot read Arabic script, the message can still be decoded. I can read it iconically, although not graphemically.

Figure 3-6   Two ways to "read" a stop sign: graphemically and iconically

On the exterior wall of a tiny market, across the intersection from the stop sign, and still visible from my bedroom window, is another product of literacy, this one even more complex. It communicates its message in *three* written languages—*buvez* (French, "drink"), *Coca-Cola* (English), and, alongside, the identical message in Arabic script. It also communicates its message iconically—a bright red background, with white, flowing lettering (the tail of the first capital *C* extending under -*oca* and the head of the second capital *C* looped through the *l* of -*ola*), underscored by the stylized white wave of varying widths.

On the same exterior wall, under the Coca-Cola sign, is a metal box: its size, shape, color (yellow), and other physical attributes (a keyhole, enabling it to remain locked, and an ever-open slot) sending its message—*public mailbox*—to anyone in Morocco who can read neither the Arabic script above the slot nor the French word *poste* under the slot.

Kittycorner from the market, alongside the house, is a small pharmacy, announcing itself both iconically and graphemically on

Figure 3-7 The two signs combine 3 languages for a graphemic reading and a single design for an iconic reading.

a sign standing perpendicular to the street. Underneath the Arabic script is a green even-sided cross and green crescent, the symbol of medical care throughout the Arabic-speaking world, and below the cross and crescent is a red arrow, pointing toward the entrance to the pharmacy.

These examples are typical of products of literacy in Morocco in that they *layer* symbolic systems, as reflective of a multilingual and multiliterate society, yet with a segment that is monolingual and nonliterate. Public and commercial messages read iconically and in Arabic script, like the stop sign and pharmacy sign; iconically and in Arabic and French scripts, like the mailbox; and iconically and in Arabic, French, and a third script, like the Coca-Cola sign, although it's fair to argue that *Coca-Cola* no longer counts as English.

By some estimations, only half of Moroccans are literate, the older generations having grown up in a world where literacy belonged to select males trained in traditional Islamic schools, whose goal was committing to memory the entire Quran (Wagner *et al.*, 1986). Yet today, with universal education mandated by the Moroccan government, younger generations—both boys and girls—are literate or becoming so.

Walk into any *PTT*, offering postal, telephone, and telegraphic services, and you can see the generational difference. Younger people help their parents and grandparents negotiate the demands of an increasingly literate world, as they send and receive telegraphic messages and packages requiring customs documentation. And they help with the technology of literacy, such as fax machines and telephone dials. (No *PTT*s have computer terminals yet, but that will come.)

Literacy in contemporary Morocco is embraced even by those who are not themselves literate, particularly because of the importance in their lives of the sacred scripture of the Quran. The word *Allah* or a short scripture, written in elaborate calligraphy, may adorn a living room wall, framed as a work of art. Writing may grace the bumper or windshield of a bus or transport truck, along with a stylized hand of *Fatima*, to give the driver *barakat* ("grace," or "good luck"). Miniature scriptures might be worn, around the neck, in tiny silver cylinders or leather pouches to protect the wearer.

In urban Casablanca, bookstores abound. Unlike an earlier time, when a bookstore would carry only books on religion, Islamic law (*sharia*), or Arabic grammar, contemporary Moroccan bookstores carry fiction and nonfiction, travel books with beautiful photographs and slick covers, posters, postcards, magazines, school supplies, and even children's books, printed in French or Arabic, or both. The bookstore *Carrefour* (*Crossroads*) in the Maarif, like others in Casablanca catering to an increasingly literate and sophisticated clientele, even holds readings by visiting authors.

News shops in the larger cities—Casablanca, Rabat, Fez, Marrakesh, Tangier—carry a variety of French- and Arabic-language newspapers, published in Morocco, as well as newspapers in German, Spanish, English, and Arabic flown in from other countries. Down the street from the apartment building where my family and I once lived in the Gautier section of Casablanca, "my" shop carries ten or so different daily foreign newspapers, among them the English-language *Herald Tribune*, printed in Paris and flown to Morocco, arriving by late afternoon every day. While it may be foreigners like me who buy the *Tribune*, most of the clientele of the shop is Moroccan, shopping for something to read.

BACKDROP FOR SELECTIVE EDUCATION

Certain aspects of Moroccan society help provide the context for understanding the Casablanca American School. Among them are these: it is largely multilingual and multicultural; there is an increasing value placed on education and technology; and a segment of the population has the means to provide educationally for their children.

Two hundred or so Moroccan students, termed *host country nationals*, comprise about half the student body of CAS, and they come from homes wealthy enough to pay a tuition the equivalent of elite private school tuition in the United States. This amount, about $7,000 dollars a year, would be beyond the reach of most middle-income American parents, whether living in the States or abroad.

The other half of the student body is from 20 or so different countries around the world. And only a fraction of this half is from the United States. (Here, for counting purposes, the distinction is made between *Americans* and *third country nationals*.) Quite a few Indian families, living in Casablanca for generations and belonging to a close-knit community, send their children to the school. And these children are also considered third country nationals, since they are not Muslim, by religion, and are, therefore, not citizens of

Figure 3-8   Entrance to the Casablanca American School

Morocco. Other school parents are in Morocco as employees of multinational companies, like Goodyear and Siemens, which pay their employees' children's school tuition as part of a benefits package. These children might well be attending elite private schools wherever they lived.

Other children enrolled at the school belong to diplomatic families, posted at the various foreign consulates in Casablanca. Still others are the children of teachers working at the school. As an employment benefit to its teachers, the school waives the full tuition for one child and half tuition for a second child. In another context, these latter children might not be enrolled in so expensive a private school. Such was certainly the case for my child during the time I spent at the school in the late 1980s.

The economic profile of CAS students and their families is important in understanding the school, but it can also be misleading. Aspects of my description may conjure up images of a rich kids' school: spoiled children being catered to by an administration afraid of losing their parents' hefty tuition. Such a characterization would be unfair and inaccurate.

Parents of children at the school, while treated with respect and welcomed into the school community—to consult with their children's teachers, chaperon school activities, and work for the school through the Parent–Teachers' Organization—soon learn that everyone is treated equally and the school rules apply to all, including them and their children. Children who are not serious about their studies or who flout the rules don't stay long: unsuccessful counseling and unheeded warnings are followed by explusion, whether the child is the son of a government minister, foreign diplomat, or teacher at the school.

This aspect of the school culture largely stems from the administrative style and personality of the school director, an American from the Boston area, who—in a little over a decade—has nursed the school from a small operation that was academically and financially shaky, holding classes in an old house near the center of Casablanca, to the academically respected and financially solvent operation it is today, settled into its modern, new campus in *Californie*. Inherently respectful of all members of the school community, from the cafeteria cooks to the board of directors, the director—tough and demanding, yet caring—privileges no one.

While the director's administrative style creates stresses in a school community in which people of importance—foreign diplomats, local elites, and U.S. expatriots with egos inflated from living in third world countries—are accustomed to getting what they want by virtue of wanting it, it is ultimately the only viable way to do business. And, despite the stresses, this administrative style promotes a school culture infused with fairness, respect, and equality.

While lightly subsidized by the U.S. government—receiving a small annual grant, usually about $30,000, as an overseas school educating United States nationals—the Casablanca American School is neither owned nor run by the American government. Nor is it run exclusively *for* American children, who, in fact, normally make up no more than about 10 percent of the student body.

Nevertheless, an occasional American parent or two, new to the country and the school, mistakenly assume that it's "their" school. Acting as if they have authority by virtue of being well-placed Americans, they generally assume that only they know anything about education, and they condescend to the administrative staff, many of whom have spent years building the school into what it is today. Fortunately, the loyalty, commitment, and respect of the school community—other parents and faculty—is such that these few "ugly" Americans become marginalized. The damage they do gets repaired by others who remain behind, and the work of the school goes on.

The school, in fact, operates according to a nonprofit charter, granting ownership to the full-time faculty and parents of CAS students, whoever they happen to be at any given time. This constitutes the operational framework, despite the fact that the school's curriculum *is* basically American, many of its teachers are U.S. hires, its teaching aids and textbooks are bought in the States, and English is the medium of instruction.

According to school bylaws, the U.S. Consul General is the head of the board of directors, but the other board members are elected by the community of parents whose children attend the school. Moroccan parents, as well as parents of third country nationals, are regularly elected to the board for three-year terms.

CAS is part of a loose federation of American schools in Morocco, the other two being the Rabat American School, 50 kilometers to the north, and the much smaller Tangier American School, in the northernmost Moroccan city. While each one functions independently, they acknowledge their sisterhood by competing with each other in sports or collaborating occasionally on professional matters such as curriculum development.

Through various other professional affiliations, the Casablanca American School situates itself internationally, and not just as Moroccan-based or U.S.-connected. CAS teachers and administrators actively participate in MAIS, the Mediterranean Association of International Schools, a professional organization with member schools from Spain and Portugal, in the west, to Tunisia, in the east. MAIS member schools work together on educational policy and convene annually at a conference hosted by a member school.

CAS also holds membership in the European Council of International Schools and sends its administrators and a score of teachers to the ECIS conference, held annually in a major European city, such as Rome, Frankfurt, or Madrid. The year I was a teacher there, the conference convened in Paris.

In Casablanca, third country nationals have few choices if they want their children educated in other than an Arabic-medium curriculum, and, in fact, they have *no* choice other than CAS, if they want English-medium schooling. Moroccan families, on the other hand, have a variety of choices. For their children, they could choose French government schools (French-medium schooling through a countrywide and well-regarded *lycée* system), or, less visible, Spanish government schooling (Spanish-medium).

Figure 3-9   Casablanca American School, from the playground

Occasionally, wealthy Moroccan families send their adolescent children to European boarding schools, although Moroccans must surely score high in any ranking of a society's emotional attachment to its children and sending them away to school seems out of character.

Generally, for Moroccan parents, an obvious choice for their children would be Arabic-medium schooling, but the national (public) schools suffer from a reputation, perhaps deserved, of being harshly disciplinarian and hopelessly archaic in methodology, with rote memorization and oral recitation still the norm. Thus, for education conscious parents, even those of moderate means, the public schools become increasingly unacceptable, and educational entrepeneurs are stepping in to provide alternatives. By catering to a market that can pay tuition and is attracted by computer literacy, multilingualism, and quality education for their children, Moroccan private schools are growing in number in neighborhoods all over Casablanca. These new private schools meet the educational needs of some local families, but not all.

CHOICE OF THE AMERICAN SCHOOL

Why then would some Moroccans send their children to an English-medium school, culturally associated with the United States? This, when they themselves may never have been to the States, and, in some cases, are not themselves fluent in English? My answers are cobbled together from bits and pieces of conversations held and/or overheard, constructed according to my interpretations:

◇ Prestige is attached to what is American, and parents construe *American* to mean superior quality and effectiveness.

◇ American education, particularly American higher education, has a worldwide reputation for excellence; and this general sense spills over to *all* American academic institutions.

◇ Status is attached to sending one's children to a school where other socially and politically prominent families send *their* children.

◇ Rote learning, harsh discipline, and authoritarian teachers are traditionally associated with Moroccan schooling. And more educated Moroccan parents understand these to be negative factors in the educational process.

◇ French schools are perceived to be a colonial legacy, and, there, some Moroccan parents think their children would be treated as "second class."

◇ Moroccans sense that English is the language of the future, a language their children need for economic success.

◇ Americans and American-trained teachers are thought of as good educators—open, caring, hardworking, child-oriented, fair, and democratic.

◇ American-style education is perceived to be oriented around critical thinking, a positive value parents do not associate with Moroccan education.

ADDITIONAL FACTORS IN CHOOSING "FOREIGN" SCHOOLING

While the perceptions above generally position the Casablanca American School for success, Moroccans able to afford the hefty tuition would still probably not make the decision to give their children "foreign" schooling, if it weren't for certain academic and affective factors related to the school:

◇ Although a majority of the faculty and administration are culturally and linguistically different, they create a cultural bridge for Moroccan parents that allows them to stay connected to their children. The school culture and curriculum are infused with Moroccan history and culture, Moroccan holidays are celebrated, Moroccan dignitaries are invited to speak at school events and attend school functions, and Arabic language classes are required of all Moroccan citizens. The school culture emphasizes the "guest" status of the school in Morocco, with respect and gratitude due the host country. All in all, to gain a superior education for their children, Moroccan parents are not put in the position of "losing" their children to another culture, a price parents would consider too high to pay.

◇ Moroccan parents know that CAS graduates are admitted to well-reputed American universities—among them, UCLA, Duke, Harvard, Indiana University, NYU, USC, Purdue, Princeton, Northwestern, Swarthmore—which, in turn, validates for them the quality of a CAS education.

◇ In addition to an American high school diploma, CAS is accredited to offer the International Baccalaureate (IB). This is seen by more European-oriented Moroccan families as proof of quality, as well as affording them the option of sending their children to European universities for their higher education—for some, a less daunting prospect than sending their children so far away to the United States, a country whose urban violence and fast-paced life frightens them.

◇ The school welcomes all parents as participating members of the school community, as responsible in their children's learning. Parents are invited to visit their child's class, consult with their child's teacher, and participate in the life of the school. For some parents, this status as a participant in their child's schooling, while culturally new, attracts them.

◇ The physical structure of the school is new and impressive. Won by a French architect with long-standing ties to Morocco, the design competition for the new campus was international and juried; and the winning design reflects a twenty-first-century appreciation of traditional Islamic architecture, with its arches, courtyards, tiles, and flowing space. Overall, the school physically identifies itself as culturally and permanently bound to its geographical location. It is not transplanted from the States; it is *of* Morocco.

◇ CAS has a science laboratory, art facilities, a soccer field and basketball court, a well-equipped computer laboratory, and a well-stocked library, as well as attractive classrooms. Even parents in so-called developed countries would be impressed by the school's resources and physical surroundings.

◇   Classes are small and children get individual attention. When problems arise, a child's parents are notified and asked in for consultation. It's no surprise that Moroccan parents value—and feel honored by—this partnership arrangement with the school.

◇   A large number of Moroccans are employed by the school—in both professional and nonprofessional positions—an integrating factor for successful relations between the school and the larger community. The school business manager, some of the classroom teachers, and the Arabic teachers are Moroccan; the multilingual reception staff and some of the administrative assistants are Moroccan; the cooks, gardeners, and janitorial staff are Moroccan. More importantly, from a Moroccan perspective, there is no two-tier system of benefits and remuneration, one for "foreign" hires and another for "local" hires. That means that a Moroccan teacher receives the same salary and benefits as a teacher recruited and hired in the States; the only difference is that foreign hires receive round-trip airfare (for each two-year contract) and housing or a housing subsidy.

◇   Given the size of the student body—about 400—the school staff is impressively large. CAS employs a librarian, a nurse, a full-time counselor, art and music teachers, a physical education staff, a cafeteria staff, a school bus driver, a registrar, a multilingual reception staff, a business manager, as well as credentialed teachers, most with previous international experience.

◇   With the tone set by the director and his wife, CAS teachers hired in the States work at minimizing their role as outsiders. The teachers do not live sumptuously, in part because they cannot afford to. If they own cars, the cars are local ones, bought used, and bear Moroccan license plates. In other words, no one would mistake these teachers for foreign diplomats, who live well and can be spotted a kilometer away, driving shiny, big, imported cars sporting bright yellow diplomatic plates. Neither do the American teachers have privileges at the U.S. Embassy Commissary in Rabat, where American diplomats buy their Cheerios and Jiffy peanut butter, crunchy or smooth. Overall, the teachers' lifestyle, plus their efforts in learning French/Arabic and dedicating their vacation time to seeing Morocco, impress Moroccan parents.

In ways both tangible and subtle, the school culture displays its openness to Morocco. Simultaneously, it offers positive aspects of another culture and place. From a stance of respect and accommodation, CAS invites parents and children in without needing to shed their own cultural identities. Moroccans see the school as American–Moroccan. They also see it as international, as everyone's school, belonging to no one cultural group.

FACTS ABOUT THE CASABLANCA AMERICAN SCHOOL

To get an overall sense of the Casablanca American School, it is useful to look at the way CAS bills itself:

Organization: CAS is governed by a seven-member Board of Directors, elected by the Casablanca American School Association. The Association is comprised of the parents and full-time faculty. The school has a director, deputy director (who also coordinates the International Baccalaureate), lower school principal, registrar, business manager, administrative and financial assistants, receptionists, secretaries, a school nurse, librarians, and resource specialists. The upper school (high school) has tutors, or mentors, assigned to every grade level, who serve as guidance counselors.

There is also a disciplinary council, composed of staff and students, a student council, and an active parent–teacher association. The school is accredited by the New England Association of Schools and Colleges.

Curriculum: The program of studies is fixed for all students, with certain course selections available in grades 11 and 12. Instruction is in English. French is a mandatory second language in grades 2–12, and Arabic is mandatory for host country nationals (Moroccan citizens), and is offered to other Arabic speakers.

Lower (elementary) school classes are self-contained. Each lower school teacher is assisted by either a full-time or part-time teaching intern or a classroom aide. ESL specialists offer additional instruction, as do PACE (reading) teachers. In addition to the IB (International Baccalaureate) Program, AP (Advanced Placement) courses are offered. Computer instruction is given to students in grades 1–12, with separate computer laboratories scheduled. Music and art are offered to grades K–12. Physical education, utilizing the gym and sports field, is offered to all grades, and formal health classes are given to upper school students.

After-school sports activities, such as swimming and track, utilize a pool and outdoor track at a nearby sports complex.

Admissions and Testing: CAS is a university preparatory school. Admission is based on math and English entrance exams (if students have already studied English), previous school records, and a personal interview, when possible. Readiness tests are given to preschoolers, ages 3–5. Results on French and/or Arabic exams contribute to the admissions profile and determine placement in either Francophone or non-Francophone classes and Arabic courses. Grade-level promotion is not automatic.

PSAT, SAT, and TOEFL exams are given to students in the upper school. Recent CAS graduates have been accepted at Duke, Princeton, Boston College, College of William & Mary, Hofstra, University of Virginia, Harvard, Boston University, University of Michigan, University of Connecticut, UCLA, Haute Etude de Commerce/Switzerland, and Sherbrooke and Laval Universities/Canada.

Faculty: There are 53 full-time and 11 part-time faculty/administrative staff members, including 43 from the United States, UK, Canada, Australia, and New Zealand; 11 from Morocco; and 10 from various other countries. All have university degrees, with 13 holding Master's degrees and 2 Ph.D.s. A high percentage of foreign hires stay beyond their initial contracts, with a number renewing three or four times.

Enrollment: The student–teacher ratio is 7.5 to 1. Class sizes range from 11 students to a class maximum of 22.

INVISIBLE ASPECTS OF LIFE AT THE CASABLANCA AMERICAN SCHOOL

What may not come through in this litany of facts are several aspects of CAS life:

◇ The school is highly organized; the curriculum, highly structured. While this aspect of CAS life would not appeal to a teacher who prefers a more *laissez-faire* atmosphere, or who feels that she/he wants more independence in matters of curriculum and scheduling, it is perhaps key to the success of a school with so many faculty, staff, and students from so many different countries, from different cultural backgrounds, and from different educational systems.

◇ The task is enormous: take children who may speak no English at all, some of whom may come from educational backgrounds stressing rote learning, and who—once fluent—may speak English only during

Figure 3-10   Pre-first class of mostly five-year olds

school hours, *and* prepare them in a few short years for Harvard, Princeton, Duke, or other American institutions of higher education. And to do it while fostering the development of not just "brains" but whole individuals, who need to also value sports, art, and music, and mature as responsible and respectful people. It is no wonder that a CAS school day is full and intensive.

◇ With the reputation for success the school has built over the past decade, there are more children applying for admission than there are places. As a result, the administration can afford to be increasingly selective. (According to its charter, CAS cannot, however, refuse to accept expatriot Americans.) Applicants for whom CAS is the school of last resort, those with abysmal school records elsewhere, are not admitted. Only children who have a strong chance of success in a high-powered college preparatory program such as CAS's are admitted. (The other qualifying factor here is that siblings of children already at the school are given priority.)

◇ As a component of promoting children's success, and partly as a result of my urging several years ago, children with no English are now rarely newly admitted to CAS in grade 1. The current policy is that children can enter in nursery or kindergarten (ages 3–4), where they have time to gain English fluency *before* the curriculum "requires" literacy, or they can enter in the second or third grade, after gaining literacy in their first language. Either point of entry avoids putting children—and their teachers—in the pressurized position of concentrating on both language *and* literacy, with the need to construct both, practically from scratch, in a very few short months. The earlier experience was that for some children the time was too short; yet more time in grade 1 for more language and literacy meant that a child didn't "pass"—a report card result that some parents did not understand or accept. The current policy circumvents the problem.

A CLOSE-KNIT STUDENT BODY

Although some children come and go, especially those whose parents have short-term diplomatic and professional postings to Casablanca, many CAS students are together from nursery school to high school graduation. Ties formed among these students are strong and lifelong. You can imagine the grief when tragedy strikes, as it did between my two extended stays in Casablanca, when Rachid, a student at CAS since early childhood and then a senior, was killed in a motorcycle accident.

One medium for the outpouring of grief following Rachid's death became *The Cobra*, the student newspaper. A sampling (Vol. 5/2) captures the strong sense of shared history:

> . . . Rachid will always be living in our hearts, and we will never forget his incredible sense of humor. He always cracked jokes in most unexpected situations, and always found a way to keep a cheerful atmosphere around him. We will never forget this brother of ours, who some of us have known for more than ten years. May God have mercy on his soul, and may God give strength to his unfortunate family (p. 3).
> —Othman Laraki

> [on the CAS track team winning a meet soon after Rachid's death] . . . "I think we loved Rachid so much that we ran like hell! We're all going to remember this track meet," states seventh grader Marouane Fares. The desire to win for Rachid was incredibly strong, and this was what led the CAS team to such a victory . . . (p. 1).
> —Houssam El Bassunie

> . . . we will each remember [Rachid] through memories from the past twelve years. These memories are part of each individual. This is why I do not wish to recount mine—I wish to keep them and cherish them forever alone . . . We must remember that what has happened, however tragic and woeful it may be, is simply a part of life. I say this without really believing it, simply wishing to believe. We must help each other surmount this tragedy we have not yet overcome (p. 2).
>
> —Driss Benkirane

> . . . Perhaps as Oum-Hani [a classmate] suggested to me, "It is best to pretend Rachid has gone on a long journey somewhere and that he will come back some day." Deep inside, however, I know that physically he will never come back to us. He remains, nevertheless, and will remain forever in my heart and mind. The joys we have been through, the childish disputes we have had, the moments of wild laughter, the moments of stupidity, the moments of true friendship—all these I strive to revive from the depth of my memories, that they may shine in bright radiance in my mind, bringing me ever closer to the Rachid I knew, who now remains, just as [A. E.] Housman's "Athlete Dying Young," immortal in his youth (p. 6).
>
> —Hatim Belyamani

Perhaps because I have known some of these children for most of their lives and followed their development, I am awed by their growing sense-of-self, by their successes. Awed even by the content and form of their expression, as sampled through these excerpts. For all four of these young men, English is the third language, at least. And their accomplishments extend beyond language and literacy. Hatim, for instance, is a gifted pianist. At the time this book goes to press, he is in his junior year at Harvard, double majoring in math and music.

◆ REFERENCES

Ardizzone, T. (1992). *Larabi's ox: Stories of Morocco*. Minneapolis: Milkweed Editions.

Bowles, P. (1993). The baptism of solitude. In *Too far from home: The selected writings of Paul Bowles*. Hopewell, NJ: Ecco Press.

Ellingham, M. & McVeigh, S. (1985). *The rough guide to Morocco*. London and New York: Routledge & Kegan Paul.

Heath, S. B. (1980, Winter). The functions and uses of literacy. *Journal of Communication, 30*, 123–133.

Szwed, J. F. (1981). The ethnography of literacy. In M. F. Whiteman (Ed.), *The nature, development, and teaching of written communication*, Vol. 1 (pp. 13–23). Hillsdale, NJ: Erlbaum.

Wagner, D. A., Messick, B. M., & Spratt, J. (1986). Studying literacy in Morocco. In B. Schieffelin & P. Gilmore (Eds.), *The acquisition of literacy: Ethnographic perspectives* (pp. 233–260). Norwood, NJ: Ablex.

◆ THOUGHT STARTERS
for reflection, journal writing, and/or discussion:

1. What aspects of your culture/place might strike a foreigner as contradictory or "strikingly" juxtaposed?

2. How have the literacy patterns of Morocco changed? How does this compare to literacy changes in your culture?

3. Think about the scene at the flower stall as metaphor. What aspects of life in your culture involve negotiation?

4. Americans often view their public schools as hopelessly ineffective. Yet American educational methodologies and research are often admired and emulated by others. How do you explain this contradiction?

◆ PROJECT STARTERS
for writing and research:

1. Write a brief essay in which you describe the "material culture of literacy" in your community. Include details of a product of literacy with layered symbolic systems; bring it to your classmates' attention, and explain the systems.

2. Following the format used to present facts about the Casablanca American School, describe a school you know well. Add an analysis of why (or not) parents might choose this school for their children.

3. Write a brief ethnography of your own experience with a second language. Compare the Moroccans' success with other languages to that of your own.

4. The Casablanca American School prefers to admit ESL children either very early (before first grade) or several years later (after they acquire literacy in their first language). Why this approach? Research the optimal times to begin ESL instruction.

Chapter Four

Reading Teacher-Stories: Keys to Classroom Success

As professionals, as teachers, we listen to and read, not only the stories children write and tell, but the stories children are. We listen to how children talk to each other and to us; we observe them writing, responding, manipulating, contemplating. And, based on that listening and observing—that reading of each child-story—we make decisions about how Ruben, Sonia, and Jesse are progressing and how to best further each one's learning.

—Anne Haas Dyson,
Research Currents

TWO TEACHERS

Dyson must be talking about teachers like Melanie and Eileen. Over the weeks I spend in their classrooms at the Casablanca American School, I watch as they tailor their talk, their actions, their teaching to each child. With fascination, I watch as they read the unique story each child is.

Although I never catch it on camera, Eileen and Melanie move about the classroom with eyes in the back of their heads, their keen perception sweeping the landscape of learning like a radar screen. While focusing on one child, they register the needs of each of the others. And then, seamlessly, they weave each child, each child's uniqueness, into the tapestry that becomes the whole.

To better understand how Melanie and Eileen do what they do, I set out to read the unique stories *they* are, to read *their* stories.

◇ MELANIE

Hopping Like a Bunny, Whirling Like a Dervish

The first day I enter her kindergarten classroom, Melanie is Peter Rabbit, hopping across the room. By the time I find a little chair and sit down at eye level with her mostly four-year-olds, she is crawling under Farmer McGregor's garden gate. The kids' attention is riveted on her; no little eyes stray, even to watch a stranger enter their space.

Short and round, with tan skin, sheeny black hair, and dark, almond-shaped eyes, Melanie is perpetually in motion, sometimes hopping like a bunny, more often whirling like a dervish. She crawls on the floor, she climbs up on a chair, she playacts, she dons a cape and hat. A master of voices and with costumes ready, Melanie pulls classroom "lessons" out of children's stories, like rabbits out of a hat. She's Little Red Riding Hood, walking through the forest; she's Grandma, lying in bed with her nightcap on; she's the big bad wolf, knocking on Grandma's door. And the kids interact with these characters and role-play them too.

In Melanie's classroom, her children's days are filled with language and literacy moments:

◇   Tomo, largely silent but ever observant, proudly delivers a note from his mother to Melanie. As Tomo watches her every move, Melanie reads the note, a smile breaking out on her face as the message of the note comes through. She thanks Tomo for the note and hands it to her aide, saying, "Here, Miss Karima, read the note that Tomo brought from his mother." Tomo beams.

◇   Sara, effusive and full of smiles, finishes her snack and goes to the reading circle, stretching out on her stomach with *The Very Hungry Caterpillar*, a book Melanie has read to the class that morning. As Sara turns each page slowly and deliberately, she speaks under her breath, telling herself the story as she goes. Joining her on the carpet, Melanie looks up at the others, noisily finishing their snacks, and says, "Excuse me, could we have some quiet. Sara and I are reading."

◇   Zak goes to the board and laboriously forms some letters while his classmates are cleaning up for the day. I notice Zak and ask what he's writing, since he's standing between me and the board and I can't see. Zak remains quiet, but Sara, who often puts herself in charge, steps forward to answer my question. Her eyes twinkling, she tells me that Zak can't write. From the look on her face, I can tell that she thinks she's got one up on Zak. Zak ignores us both and keeps on writing.

Born into a Chinese-American family in San Francisco, Melanie grew up speaking English. Like the parents of Richard Rodriguez, her parents spoke to her in *foreigner* English, fearful that others would not accept their children as American if they spoke their ancestral language. Melanie regrets the loss.

After graduating from San Jose State University in California, Melanie began teaching in the Bay area, in upper-middle-class Santa Clara. Then, feeling she owed something back, she shifted over to a school in a predominantly Hispanic area, one served by the San Jose Unified School District. There, she team-taught with a Japanese-American colleague, fluent in Spanish, from whom she says she began to truly understand the intellectual and cultural richness of bilingual education.

Although she gained fluency in Spanish, Melanie didn't feel qualified to teach Spanish language arts in a middle school in the area, a position she was next asked to take. Declining the middle school job, she was assigned to kindergarten. Upon hearing her assignment, she cried, she said, afraid she wouldn't be any good at it, afraid she wouldn't like it. Now she says she can't imagine teaching anything *but* kindergarten.

Now in her fifteenth year of teaching, Melanie is in her fifth year at the Casablanca American School. For the first three years at CAS, Melanie's husband Casey was her aide. How odd—and how interesting—Melanie thought it must have seemed for students and parents to see them working together as a team, yet with the female in a position of authority. In a country where the scripts of women's lives are still written by their fathers and husbands, almost never by the women themselves, here was a man working as his wife's assistant. Melanie thinks it was valuable for the children to see.

When an art position opened, Casey moved over to the art department. Then Karima, a young Moroccan mother of two small children, came on as Melanie's aide. Tall and pretty, her head covered with springy brown corkscrew curls, Karima has an open, smiling face, matched by an energetic disposition.

Karima speaks fluent English, having lived in Minnesota for a number of years, while her husband, also Moroccan, completed his graduate studies. Karima models Melanie's behavior with the children, as a result of Melanie's care in bringing Karima in on planning, but also as a result of Karima's own keen intellect. Watching Melanie and Karima work together in the classroom is like watching a ballet duet. Melanie sweeps, Karima swoops. Melanie bends, Karima bows. Syncopated motion.

Lessons-That-Don't-Seem-Like-Lessons

On another day, Melanie is in the classroom reading–talking–acting *Are You My Mother?* by Dr. Seuss, the story of a newly hatched baby bird who asks the most unlikely animals if they're his mother. Huge drawings of the story characters line the walls. Sitting in the reading circle, Melanie's four-year-olds respond enthusiastically to her invitation to help read the story—*Come on, help me say that.* The story structure immediately reveals itself to them, as they anticipate the question–answer refrain, chanting it like a mantra at just the right moment. *Are you my mother? No, I am not your mother . . . Are* **you** *my mother? No, I am **not** your mother.* To everyone's great relief, the baby bird finds his mother.

On a second run through the story, Melanie points to specific words in the big book. *This word says SNORT,* Melanie asserts, as she traces her finger along the curves of the *S*, down the pillars and angular crossbar of the *N*, around the circular *O*, and so on. Later, as recess begins, Zak steals up to the big book, still standing on its easel, and traces the word with his stubby little finger.

After recess, the kids choose puppets from the treasure chest and take turns acting out the story, with Melanie and Karima launching the activity by modeling the kids' roles. The performance begins. *Are you my mother? . . . No, I am not your mother . . .* with each kid raising the volume on the word *not.*

Everyone wants the next turn . . . calling out *Miss Melanie, me! No, me! Miss Melanie, me, me!* When Melanie chants *If you say me, me, me, it won't be thee, thee, thee!* they stop jockeying for turns, understanding Melanie's admonition. Their eagerness to participate doesn't diminish, but the two taking their turn do encounter less static.

The baby bird's reunion with his mother segues into the *family* as topic and Melanie, now the music director, leads the pint-size choir in a song about families. Following Dalila's eyes as she and her classmates sing, I realize she's looking at the wall, and I turn to find the lyrics to the song on a poster just behind me. I locate the line and move my finger along to the singing. When Dalila and I next make eye contact, she nods in approval, pleased with my astuteness.

Melanie says that later in the year, she'll add more poster lyrics around the room as the kids learn more songs. And when she asks them what they want to sing, they'll probably all run to hug the lyrics of their favorite song, like last year's class did. *Hugging songs!* I say to myself, as I make a mental match between Melanie's children and the women of the Indian Chipko movement, hugging trees.

After the sing-along, the kids haul plastic buckets of crayons to the tables to draw pictures of their own families, chattering away in English, French, and Arabic as they draw and color. Tomo, the only speaker of Japanese in the class, is the quietest, but his quietness seems more personality than hesitance in English.

One child asks Melanie *which* family to draw. Reading each child-story, Melanie, knowing the child's father has two wives and two households of children, tells her to draw *all* her brothers and sisters if she'd like. The child, seeming relieved of the burden of making distinctions she'd be uncomfortable making, bends intently over her paper, producing a many-figured drawing that takes up the whole page.

As the children finish their drawings, they dictate the name of each person to Karima and Melanie, who act as their scribes and add the names to the appropriate figures on the page. One more scribe is needed, and I am pressed into service.

The seamlessness of events and tasks in Melanie's classroom awes me once again. Everything seems fortuitous, but, of course, these lessons-that-don't-seem-like-lessons don't *just happen.* They are meticulously planned by an imaginative and deeply perceptive teacher who understands how children learn and how each of her children learns, who understands what each child needs and is ready for.

These lessons-that-don't-seem-like-lessons are planned by someone who knows how to create a domain for language and literacy learning. By someone who knows that the domain for language and literacy learning, both as context and process, is simultaneously created and negotiated through talk.

The children, of course, don't know they are *learning.* They don't need to know. They think their job is to have fun; they love Melanie and Karima, and they wake up each morning, their parents say, barely able to wait to come to school.

Little Distinction Between ESL and Mainstream

This year Melanie is arranging her schedule differently, seeing her eighteen kinder kids in separate half-day sessions. Nine of her kids come from 8:30 to 11:30; the other nine, from 12:00 to 3:00. For singing and sharing, the two groups overlap from 11:30 to 12:00. Melanie prefers this to the old schedule, when all the kids were together for a half-day, because now she can focus better on each child. This must mean that, before, she had other duties during the half-day she wasn't teaching kindergarten, since she is full-time at CAS. I didn't think to ask.

In Melanie's morning class, only two of the nine children come from homes where some English is spoken. One of these two is Iraqui; the other has one Canadian parent, one Lebanese. Four of the other seven kids are Moroccan, with Arabic, or French *and* Arabic, spoken at home. Of the remaining three, one is from Japan, one is Serbian, and one is French-speaking Swiss.

All but one of the nine morning kids entered CAS at the nursery level, which means they already have a year of English-medium schooling behind them by the time I arrive to join them. The Swiss child, however, is brand-new to English, yet the instructional scaffolding that Melanie constructs for each child—what the child is invited to do and the assistance she's given to do it—integrates the Swiss child into the whole, enabling her to be a participating member of the class and, to the casual observer, indistinguishable from the other children.

In Melanie's afternoon class, only one of the nine is a first-language speaker of English, a child whose parents teach at the school. Seven of the nine are Moroccan, with Arabic, or French and Arabic, spoken at home. The other child might be bilingual—her father is an English speaker, but she lives with her Arabic-speaking mother.

Four of the nine afternoon kids are in their second year at CAS, having entered at the nursery level, which is also a half-day program. The other five, four of whom are totally new to English, are brand-new to CAS and in their first year of schooling anywhere.

Despite this newness to English and even newness to schooling, the children engage and are engaged in their classroom surroundings. As Melanie moves the children from one activity to another, little eyes focus on the task at hand. Their smiles, gestures, and actions coordinate with language. Nobody gets lost. Nobody is left behind.

In a classroom where new tasks build on old ones, where the groundwork is meticulouly laid for new challenges, I see no bewilderment, no blank stares, no looks of incomprehension on little faces. No tears, no clinging to caregivers as children are walked to the classroom and hugged goodbye at the door. Melanie's masterful interweaving of stories, tasks, singing, play—all together—carry the linguistic, literacy, and cognitive load that these four-year-olds can turn into understanding, turn into learning. And the interweaving "happens" through talk.

◇◇ EILEEN

Creating a Holding Place for Language Yet to Come

In Eileen's pull out ESL class of first graders, Edward is at the felt board in front of his five classmates. He rummages among the cutout characters on the table to find the ones he needs to tell the story of the gingerbread man. Thin and frail, with blond hair and translucent skin, Edward is six years old, a speaker of French, and in his first year at CAS. On this day, he is in his *third week* of English-language immersion.

Eileen stands to the side, smiling encouragement at Edward's undertaking. Like a stage manager, Eileen cues him into his performance. *And then . . . and then . . . what happens next? . . . and then . . .* . Although shy, Edward doesn't seem ill at ease. Eileen's easy manner and flow of playful language put no one on the spot, let no attempt end in failure.

As Edward locates the cutout he wants next and adds it to the board—left to right, back and forth—he displays knowledge of the story Eileen has just acted–read–told the class. Maybe he knows the story in French, maybe not. First the old woman in her kitchen, then opening the oven door, then the gingerbread man jumping out, then running down the lane chased by the old woman . . . *pant, pant.*

With so little English to draw from, Edward hits on a clever strategy for managing his performance. Each time he presses a cutout to the board, he sings the ditty he's appropriated from Eileen's rendition of the story—*Run, run, as fast as you can. You can't catch me, I'm the gingerbread man!* Up goes the third cutout, out comes the refrain. Up goes the fourth cutout, out comes the refrain. *Good job, Edward*, extolls Eileen, barely able to contain her amusement after the fifth time.

With the song, Edward creates a holding place for language yet-to-come, masterfully pressing the refrain into service as a transition between story segments, now represented by the cutouts. The song will serve until other words come along to provide the cohesion Edward knows his story needs. Eileen, catching on early to Edward's plan of action, turns to me and winks, as I capture his performance on film.

As his finale, Edward exaggerates the gingerbread man entering the fox's mouth, then goes to the felt board to place these cutouts on the river. This time Edward foregoes the refrain, displaying full well that the gingerbread man's singing days are over. No more *run, run, as fast as you can*. The gingerbread man is done for.

Pantomime as Conversation

Luis's hand then shoots up with such vigor that it pulls his little body off the chair. His show of interest is a good sign, since, of the six in the class, he is the most resistant to English. Caught up in the energy around him, Luis momentarily forgets his decision not to learn English and steps up to the felt board. Once there, he remembers. Without missing a beat, Eileen steps forward and suggests he tell the story in his native Spanish.

Small, with brown hair and twinkling eyes, Luis—the Marcel Marceau of Eileen's ESL class—points to himself, as if to say *Who? Me? Are you talking to me?* Eileen, unfazed, as if pantomime were a perfectly expected half of a conversation, replies, *Sure, tell it in Spanish. We'd like that.* Luis points to himself again and closes the deal by nodding his head. *Espanish,* he says, with finality. *Yes, Spanish,* affirms Eileen. With no front teeth to stem the flow of aspiration, Luis commences his Spanish rendition of the gingerbread man story.

Across the felt board, the little old lady, the farmer, and the farm animals chase the gingerbread man, accompanied by Luis's commentary in Spanish. Accustomed to pressing other modes of communication into service whenever English-speaking isn't viable, Luis's classmates give him their attention, although no one else speaks his language.

Luis will soon, of course, speak English. In fact, when I see him a few months later, he speaks English fluently, although he holds out for several months after the Day of the Gingerbread Man. *He thinks he's stronger than I am, he thinks he can hold out*, Eileen claims

to me later, *but he doesn't know me! I'm stronger,* she says mischie-
vously, *so I and English will win.* I have no doubt. Like a siren, Eileen
will entrance Luis into English, make him forget his resistance,
make involvement with English so enticing—with stories, pictures,
play, drama, action, music, and song—that he will heed the call.

Focus on the Message

The six kids in Eileen's pull-out class are with her every morning
from 9:40 to 11:30, during the time when their more-English-fluent
classmates do language arts. Of the six, two—Joudy and Radoun—
are cousins from Syria; Edward the Clever is from France; Anna-
with-the-Pigtails is Polish; Sweet Youssef is Moroccan; and Luis-
of-the-Twinkling Eyes is from Spain. All are new to the Casablanca
American School, and to English.

As background, it may help to know that CAS has two first-
grade classes—one class (Eloise's) of nineteen children, the other
(Patricia's) of twenty-two. Half of Eileen's little ESL group comes
from Patricia's first grade class, half from Eloise's. Five of Eloise's
first-graders and six of Patricia's are also pulled out for an ESL
boost, but only for a half hour during "regular" language arts
instruction. Unlike Eileen's kids, who are brand-new to English,
these eleven are in their second year of English-medium schooling,
so the amount of assistance they are deemed to need is less. These
eleven meet daily with Karen, one of the other ESL teachers, in
two small groups.

Of the first graders who are *not* pulled out to work with either
Eileen or Karen, only two are first-language speakers of English,
one in Patricia's class, one in Eloise's. This, in effect, makes *all* first
grade instruction ESL instruction, with every lesson needing to be
designed with an eye toward English-language, as well as literacy,
development.

In fact, the whole school is an ESL school, with less than ten
percent of the entire student body native English-speaking. Yet
children graduating from CAS—those choosing to come to the
United States for higher education—are accepted at highly competi-
tive schools but that is not Eileen's and Melanie's story. But yet
again it is, since the foundation is laid by the Eileens and Melanies
in these children's lives.

Eileen—herself fluent in three languages, English, German, Arabic—is not a linguistic purist; and this is one of the many keys to

her success with the kids. For her, language serves communication. That's its function. And if, in a given situation, English, German, or Arabic won't do, she'll try a little of Edward's French or Luis's Spanish. Or, in lieu of language, she'll try pantomime or drawing. I've seen conversations between Eileen and Luis, with her speaking English to him, and him drawing pictures back to her—and with neither showing any signs that this is other than a perfectly normal conversation.

For Eileen, the message is what counts. In her home, with her own three children, you'll hear English, German, and Arabic, sometimes in the same conversation. Eileen's two older children, both teenagers, also speak French. And her little one, Ghizlane, a five-year-old, is in a bilingual school—half-day French, half-day Arabic—and she will soon also be a French speaker.

Who You Are is How You Teach And Vice Versa

Eileen's childhood language is British English, but once out of school, she moved to Germany, where she became a fluent speaker of German. Eventually, she married Ahmed, a Moroccan she met in Germany, and, with him, set up an import business in Hamburg. For a number of years, German was hers and Ahmed's common language, until she learned Moroccan Arabic and he learned English.

When their first two children approached school age, Eileen and Ahmed decided that, with a British mother and a Moroccan father, the children needed a more integrated cultural upbringing than was possible for them in Germany. In Germany—Eileen and Ahmed's thinking went—their children would either create a social identity for themselves as German—when in their home culture they were not—or an identity as *Ausländer*—which to ethnic Germans they would, in fact, be. Eileen and Ahmed felt the cultural dissonance was not what they wanted for their children, and they made the decision for Eileen and the two kids to move to Casablanca—this was before the birth of the third—while Ahmed, who still runs the business in Germany, returns to Morocco when business permits.

With Ahmed gone so much, Eileen—British and female—must navigate family life in a Muslim Arab, male-dominant culture. Short, fair, and small, but completely fluent in Arabic, Eileen can talk her way in and out of most anything. Always cheerful, witty, and capable of the most clever of repartees, Eileen usually leaves her interlocutors smiling—and, likely, minus whatever she has come for. So it is with Eileen's ESL students. She takes from them their resistance to English and leaves them smiling and speaking English. It's from this perspective that Eileen claims, at the beginning of the school year, that she'll win Luis over. That he won't be able to hold out.

Tea And Reflection

One late evening, over English tea, Eileen and I talk about our time teaching together several years earlier. As we reminisce, Eileen contemplates the mystery each child is. How teachers rarely have a chance to learn the degree of their success in reaching children, the degree to which lives are positively affected.

> *Remember little Raza* [a Kurdish child who came to CAS from Iraq immediately after a yearlong separation from her parents, trapped outside their country during Iraq's war with Iran]. *Like* [Richard] *Rodriguez* [as told in Hunger of Memory], *Raza didn't say a word in English for weeks and weeks and weeks. She gave me grey hair. Thought she'd never speak. Now, she's one of the best students in the school. She sees me and says, "Hi, Mrs. Achaoui. How are you? Remember when we did this, and this, and this!!"*

> *Zero English. That's what those second and third graders began with. Remember? We'd start off with classroom vocabulary, the stuff around us—* chair, table, book. *We'd do TPR* [the language-teaching method, Total Physical Response]. *We'd work on shapes, colors, food—to get a little vocabulary down. We'd find circles, squares, rectangles in the classroom. When I'd ask for circles, the kids'd scour the room to find circles, coming up with something like the top of the trash can, and then they'd trace it. I'd give them pictures of fruit to take home and they'd bring the fruit in. We'd make a fruit salad, remember? They'd retell the sequence—"Cut the banana, slice the apple . . . But what did we do first? Didn't we rinse our hands?" Then we'd draw our sequence on butcher paper and label the drawings. We didn't forget to eat the salad, though. Then we'd write a story about it.*

> *By 'bout February that year, we were working with books and stories. Remember* Strega Nona? *The art teacher was wonderful. She'd say, "You're working on* Strega Nona, *eh? Well, how about a big cooking pot," and she'd make a big 3–D pot out of construction paper, paper fire and all! I'd have students cutting, cutting paper to put in the pot—the "spaghetti," you know!*

Potion—*they'll never forget that word! Listen to the story, tell it, read it, tell it, and write about it. The story about Coco* [gorilla that learned sign language] *and the kittens . . . remember that one? We'd bring in Aramis* [one of the teachers who signed] *to do the sign language. Miss Morgan Went Missing—they'd actually beg for that story. Act it out, take the parts. "How would X have felt? How would Y have done that?"*

We'd pull out the vocabulary. With one story—I forget the title—we did "noisy" food and "quiet" food. We ate actual food to hear how it sounds. Then we listed which ones were noisy, which ones were quiet. I'd pull out "ings" and "eds" and we'd go over those.

*With kindergartners, remember? we'd show pictures, ask them to guess what the book was about. "What do you think will happen?" On butcher paper, we'd write each kid's name, then just a key word or two about the kid's guess. We didn't have many supplies to work with, not like now. Then we'd read the story and go back over the guesses. We'd find which ones were the same. The kids would pick out their names. Just give me a few good books, some paper and pencils. I can do just fine. When I see students a year later and they say "Mrs. Achaoui, remember when we read such and such a book?" Now **that** gives me satisfaction.*

Remember the workshop I told you about? The one Nocha [pre-first teacher] *and I did at MAIS* [Mediterranean Association of International Schools]? *The workshop on songs that're great for ESL? A teacher—don't know which school she's from—came up to me when it was over and said, "Eileen, what's wrong with you is that you're too much of an entertainer in the classroom." I was crushed—began to doubt myself. When I told Marge* [pre-first teacher] *later, she said, "Eileen, don't be silly. That's the best compliment any of us could ever get!" And Marge is right, you know.*

⟨⟨⟩ KEYS TO SUCCESS

As I reflect on Eileen and Melanie, about the essence of who they are as teachers, I read the following as keys to their success:

◇ In their classrooms, language and literacy are embedded in tasks and never isolated. Tasks always have purpose; and the focus is on communicating, on making meaning.

◇ Melanie and Eileen are not embarrassed to demonstrate to children their enthusiasm, their passion, for language and literacy. For them, presentation *is* performance, imbued with wholehearted joy.

◇ In Melanie's and Eileen's classrooms, children are *enticed* into learning.

The fun and pageantry of it all—color, music, pictures, games, puppetry, stories, songs—pull children in and sweep them off their feet.

◇ Eileen and Melanie continually adjust the framework, raise the bar, to provide what Cazden (1982) calls *scaffolded assistance*. The kids do more and more, as Eileen and Melanie lay the groundwork, orchestrate, and assist.

◇ Melanie and Eileen emphasize play. They themselves are playful, thereby diminishing the distance between themselves and their students. They joke with the kids, burst into song when the spirit moves them, and are *ever* upbeat and cheerful. They make each child feel special—valued, liked, and respected—and ever so intelligent.

◇ In Melanie's and Eileen's classrooms, reading, writing, and talking are seamlessly integrated, as urged by Harste *et al.* (1981). Melanie and Eileen work intuitively *across* the various systems of communication. Their classrooms are multimedia operations.

◇ For Eileen and Melanie, every moment is a potential learning moment. They seize the moment, whether planned or fortuitous, to move a child's learning forward. In their classrooms, it's hard to tell what is, what is not, the lesson. There are no *lesson lines*.

◇ Melanie and Eileen are willing to use any available communication means in the service of the message. If children can't say it, they can draw it or act it out. Melanie and Eileen accept what Cook–Gumperz (1975) calls *negotiability;* that is, behavior in achieving communication can always be negotiated.

◇ Eileen and Melanie accept kids as they are, where they are, with what they have. It is children that Melanie and Eileen teach, not a curriculum. They know all kids are the same and each child is different. They also know that each child is complex, and so are the contexts for emerging language and literacy.

◇ Like Langer (1986), Eileen and Melanie look for long-term results in their teaching, not overnight success.

◇ As Heath (1991) advocates, Eileen's and Melanie's classrooms are filled with talk, talk, and more talk. Melanie and Eileen talk to encourage. They talk to explain. They talk to instruct. They talk to model. They talk about talk.

This is how I read Melanie's and Eileen's teacher-stories.

◆ REFERENCES

Cazden, C. B. (1982). Adult assistance to language development: Scaffolds, models and direct instruction. In R. Parker & F. Davis (Eds.), *Developing literacy: Young children's use of language* (pp. 3–18). Newark, DE: International Reading Association.

Cook–Gumperz, J. (1975). The child as practical reasoner. In M. Sanches & B. C. Blout (Eds.), *Socio-cultural dimensions of language use* (pp. 137–162). New York: Academic Press.

Dyson, A. H. (1986). Staying free to dance with the children: The dangers of sanctifying activities in the language arts curriculum. *English Education, 18*, 135–146.

Dyson, A. H. (1990). Research currents: Diversity, social responsibility, and the story of literacy development. *Language Arts, 67/2*, 192–205.

Harste, J., Woodward, V., & Burke, C. (1991). Examining instructional assumptions. In B. M. Power & R. Hubbard (Eds.), *Literacy in process* (pp. 51–66). Portsmouth, NH: Heinemann.

Heath, S. B. (1991). A lot of talk about nothing. In B. M. Power & R. Hubbard (Eds.), *Literacy in process* (pp. 79–87). Portsmouth, NH: Heinemann.

Langer, J. A. (1986). *Children reading and writing: Structures and strategies.* Norwood, NJ: Ablex.

◆ THOUGHT STARTERS
for reflection, journal writing, and/or discussion:

1. From the anecdotal "evidence" offered in this chapter, discuss how Melanie and Eileen are able to discover "what each child needs and is ready for."

2. What is the difference between teaching "subject matter" and teaching "each child"? Which is more demanding? More effective? Must a teacher choose between the two?

3. Discuss why teacher-stories can be valuable to researchers. To other teachers. If you were writing a teacher-story of one of your early teachers, who would you choose? Why?

4. Have someone tell your group a story in a language that only the storyteller knows. Work together to retell the story. Afterwards, note the strategies useful to managing the task. Share your thoughts on the experience.

◆ PROJECT STARTERS
for writing and research:

1. Melanie's and Eileen's classes are rich in literacy experiences. Take a story or passage that would be effective in an oral reading. Develop a literacy activity related to it (for a class at any level). Explain who, what, and why.

2. Search the literature for teacher-stories. Present your findings in an annotated bibliography of the three or four you like best.

3. Spend an hour or two observing a teacher recognized as outstanding. Write a summary of your observations and draw up a list of "keys to her/his success."

4. Design a means of teaching a story to young ESL'ers. Think of creative ways the kids might use to retell the story. In Eileen's class, a felt board is used. What else might be useful?

Chapter Five

"Words in My Ears, Letters in My Head": Methods and Lessons for Language and Literacy Learning

With Marge Gruzen*

> Little children show us delightful glimpses of the growth
> of thinking, feeling, and doing. Unfortunately, they typi-
> cally give us these glimpses when our tape recorders
> are turned off, our pencils are neatly in our jars, and our
> bodies are ready for rest, recreation, or food. Researchers
> who wish to record the development of children are
> prodded by the nature of their young subjects to recon-
> sider traditional methodology . . . with the goal of
> learning more about kindergartners as writers and
> readers.
>
> —Elizabeth Sulzby,
> *Kindergartners as Writers and Readers*

LEARNING MORE ABOUT WRITERS AND READERS

Five-year-old Christina, trilingual in English, French, and Arabic,
shows me the picture she has just drawn in her pre-first class at
the Casablanca American School. Moments earlier, Christina and
her 22 classmates listened as Marge, their pre-first teacher, read *On
the Day You Were Born*. And now they are responding to Marge's
invitation to "tell your own story." Telling Christina how much I

*The chapter was written with assistance from Marge Gruzen, the pre-first grade teacher
whose reflections on teaching round out the chapter. Marge is now at the International
School of Manila, Philippines. The chapter also results from collaboration with Nocha Myers,
Eileen Achaoui, and Patricia Boisseau.

like her picture, I encourage her to tell more in writing, so I'll know "the *whole* story."

Insisting that she doesn't know how to write, I encourage her to go ahead. *I'll bet you know about writing*, I say. With her long, brown hair partially obscuring her drawing, she bends forward, and rapidly spins long lines of writing around her drawing, along the bottom of the paper, up one side, across the top, and down the other side. When she stops and looks up to catch my eye, I ask her if she'll read it to me, which she does.

Clearly knowing what it says, which I do not, since she's not using conventional letters, Christina reads her story seriously and rapidly. Curious to know how committed she is to her writing, I say I'd like to hear it again and again, since *Oh my goodness, it's such a wonderful story.* She reads it to me two more times, *exactly* the same way each time.

Although Christina's writing doesn't show evidence that she yet understands sound–letter (as symbol) correspondences, she knows that her marks on the page "say" something. As evidence of her development as not only a writer, but a writer of English, Christina's writing moves from left to right, showing that she already has the hang of the directionality of English writing, unlike the writing of Arabic (one of her home languages), which moves from right to left.

Confident that Christina has something to say that I would benefit from hearing, I give Christina's writing the respect it deserves, asking her to read it to me, since I cannot read it for myself. Given the seriousness and carefulness with which she reads it, a correspondence between meaning and her marks on the page are there for her, and it is of no consequence to her that, at the moment, they are not there for me. I would no more dismiss her as a writer than I would dismiss her as a doctor, if she said she was one and wanted to examine my "hurt" finger. I wouldn't say *You're not a real doctor and my finger isn't really hurt.* It has only taken a small boost from me for Christina to establish firmness in her conviction that her writing says what she says it says.

Vincent, a French-speaker from Belgium, now at the beginning of his second year in the school, shows no timidity about *his* writing. In large, deliberate, and conventional letters, he writes his story about the day he was born, recycling the few letters he has in his small-but-growing inventory of letters to create a myriad of meanings (Fig. 5-1). He reads his story to me several times: *You hoo, my mommy said. After, my daddy said. After, mommy said, Daddy,*

Figure 5-1   Vincent's story about the day he was born, read by Vincent as *You hoo, my mommy said. After, my daddy said. After, mommy said, Daddy, come see.*

come see. Vincent's story is secured on paper with eight bold letters and one strong dot (a period?): *V I S I S · S A C [.]*

Mira, trilingual in Arabic, French, and English, and, like Vincent, in her second year of CAS schooling, asks for an eraser to change "I WLN" to "I WAS." Then she simply crosses it out and starts again. Asking Marge to tell her the name of what she's drawn, Marge says "crib." Not satisfied, Mira says *"No, not 'crib,' but the thing you push in the hospital."* Marge says "gurney." Asking Marge to write it on a piece of paper, Mira then copies it onto her paper, to accompany her drawing of the bed-with-wheels on which she has positioned her newborn baby-self (Fig. 5-2).

Hicham, a home speaker of French and Arabic, writes a story, but lacks the confidence to read it; and Hussein, also a home speaker of Arabic and French, insists he can't remember what his writing says.

Nidal, a first language speaker of Arabic/French, who seems never to listen or pay attention, at first says he is not going to tell a story, but then ends up writing more than most of the kids. When I ask if he'll read it to me, he eagerly proceeds.

I am in Marge's classroom to learn about these kids as writers and readers. I am spending the school year in Marge's classroom, as well as in other classrooms at CAS, to learn more about the environments, and the lessons and methods, that promote language and literacy in a multilingual, multicultural setting.

Among the three instructional levels—kindergarten, pre-first, and first grade—that interest me most, only 2 of the 121 children are monolingual speakers of English. And only a handful of the other 119 have (some) English in the home. Yet for all of these children— who, as individuals, are first language speakers of Berber, German, Italian, Spanish, Polish, Chinese, French, Arabic, Dutch, Flemish, Japanese, Hindi, or Serbian, and often two or three of these languages in combination—English is the first language of literacy, the language in which they are becoming writers and readers.

What follows are segments of lessons in four of these classrooms, lessons that give a view of how language and literacy emerge in such a culturally and linguistically rich but complex setting. The segments are followed by Marge's reflections on teaching pre-first grade in such a setting. The title of the chapter comes from Christina, who, when I ask her how she knows so much about writing, tells me she has words in her ears and letters in her head. I have no doubt she does.

Figure 5-2   Mira's story about the day she was born. At Mira's request, her teacher wrote out the word *gurney* for her, and she copied it. (See next page.)

Figure 5-2 Continued

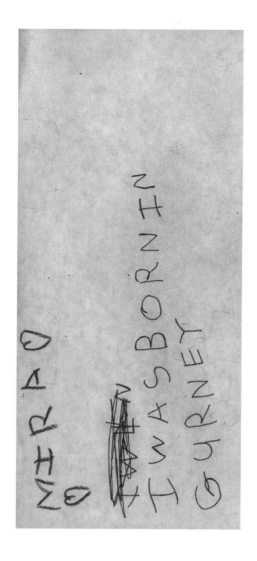

◇◇ PRE-FIRST: MARGE'S INTEGRATED UNIT, *ALL ABOUT ME*

Players

Marge starts off the day—and the school year—with play, because she thinks the kids seem reluctant to initiate play with their peers. She has them choose an activity and take it off the shelf, from among the puzzles, blocks, manipulatives, and other possibilities in the well-furnished classroom. Usually the boys play with the boys, the girls with the girls, Marge finds.

Of Marge's 23 pre-first students, mostly five-year-olds, two are "repeating" pre-first, both from Nocha's pre-first class of last year. These two are with Marge now so that they can have a change of classroom. (Nocha now has one child from Marge's last year's pre-first class.) One of the two has gone through a particularly messy divorce, Marge says. The other child, Marge suspects, has some learning disabilities.

Of the 21 others, two are beginning their first full year at CAS. One of these, Christina of the words and letters, came in during summer school. This leaves 19 who have either entered the school at the nursery or kindergarten level, which gives them one to two years of English immersion behind them, as Marge begins her school year with them. None is a monolingual English speaker. Only 4 of the 23 have some English in the home.

On one wall of the classroom is a happy face chart for especially good self-initiated jobs, such as cleaning up after play. In fact, "Good job!" is Marge's favorite phrase, and I hear it often in her classroom. On Fridays, the children who have accumulated enough happy face stickers to fill up their line on the chart get a happy face sticker to "wear" home, usually on their foreheads. Almost everyone makes it most weeks.

Team ESL

After play, Eileen, the ESL specialist, joins Marge for a 35-minute oral language development lesson. Having coordinated their plans, Eileen paves the way for Marge's unit *All About Me*, whose goals are body awareness, English-language development, and self-esteem building. Eileen reads the book, *All About Me*, and has kids represent, by drawing and coloring, the notions *wavy, curly,* and *straight, blond, black, light brown,* and *dark brown*. Then volunteers stand up, and the other kids, with their new words, describe the volunteers' hair.

Eileen and Marge work well together and respect each other's capabilities. Marge tells me later that the CAS Lower School (nursery through eighth grade), and particularly grades one through four, need more Eileens. Then each classroom could have a full-time ESL teacher team-teaching with the "regular" classroom teacher, with greater emphasis on language development. Marge feels lucky that Eileen is assigned to work "in-house" with the kindergarten and pre-first grades, at least.

At the grades above pre-first, Eileen and another ESL teacher work on a pull-out arrangement, which doesn't work as well, Marge says, as the in-class teamwork. Even with pull-out though, Eileen manages to make it work because she puts so much effort into coordinating her work with the classroom teacher, turning it into a team-teaching operation after all. I see for myself that, without this extra effort at coordination, pull-out does not contribute much to students' in-class success.

About three hours later, one of the least English-fluent children in the class says to me, as we are walking back from buddy reading time with George's fourth graders, *Your hair is wavy*, showing off his newly-acquired vocabulary. *Yes, it is*, I say. *And what color would you say it is?* I ask. *Brown and black*, he says. *Ah*, I say, *you have good eyes. Would black and brown together make it "dark brown." Hmmm, yes*, he muses.

Thinking for Yourself

Marge says that she often finds the children unaccustomed to doing much for themselves. They may drop trash and just walk away, Marge says, or spill something and watch it run. As if to verify her point, during snack time one child asks Marge to peel his banana. Marge tells the child how, and he then does it for himself. Another child says he doesn't want to finish his half-eaten peach. *Well, what might you do with it?* Marge asks. *Throw it in the garbage can*, the child concludes. *Good idea*, Marge surmises, as the child heads toward the garbage can. One of the things Marge wants the children to learn is responsibility, so lots of happy face stickers go up on the chart for responsible behavior. The kids think it's a big deal to get a happy face on Fridays.

Looking for Learning Moments

After snack time, the children head for the carpet for show-and-tell. Hicham raises his hand, volunteering to start. As he starts

Figure 5-3   Marge's pre-first class

to pull something out of his pocket, Marge stops him and asks everyone, *If it's in Hicham's pocket, is it big or little? Little,* they conclude. Hicham has a pencil sharpener in the shape of a football helmet, which he calls a "mask." Marge models the term "football helmet" as she interacts with Hicham, and he shifts from *mask* to *helmet* without missing a beat.

Marge seizes the opportunity to get the kids to extrapolate into occasions when people wear helmets, and the kids come up with "American football" and "riding a motorcycle." Hicham says he wears a helmet when he rides his bike. By association, Christina heads off-task with "I have a tricycle and I ride it." But Marge reins her back in with "We're talking about helmets."

Marge finds that show-and-tell creates lots of contexts for talking. And talking is what Marge does a lot. A large, teddy bear of a person—even-tempered, respectful, and supportive of the children—Marge keeps up a steady stream of talking. She talks to explain, she talks to motivate, she talks to express her feelings, she talks to explain her process.

Now we're going to do "Simon Says," Marge says. *I think you need to move around a bit before we get to our work.* Several kids get happy faces for being "especially good listeners."

Print Everywhere

Lined up on top of the short bookcase are 23 rectangular tupperware-type plastic boxes with lids. Each box is labeled with a child's name, and this is where the kids store their pencils, crayons, glue sticks, and scissors, when not in use. After first letting her students bring in their own boxes, Marge finally hit on the idea of buying identical ones for everybody. When the kids brought in their own, the storage boxes were all different shapes and sizes— and were unstackable—and some kids brought in ones that were much too elaborate. This way, on the solid-colored ends, Marge can tape on a label bearing each child's name. And the child has to read his or her name in order to fetch the right box.

Journaling

After show-and-tell, and Simon Says, the kids get out their journals to draw–write. If the kids ask for scribe service, Marge and Zhor, Marge's aide, will write what the kids tell them to write at the bottom of their pictures. Christina, the one with "words in her ears and letters in her head," shows me her picture. She explains that one of the buildings is her cat's house and the other is *her* house, with her cat in it. I suggest she write all of that on her paper, but she says, once again, that she can't write. I gently suggest that I'll bet she can. *Write it your way*, I say, and she says she will just as soon as she finishes coloring her picture. A few minutes later, I see her extending her meaning beyond her picture, through writing.

Positive Reinforcement

Christina takes it upon herself to tell Valerie, a little Belgian girl, that Valerie has done her picture wrong, and Christina doesn't like the picture. Marge, hearing Christina's remarks, intervenes and asks Christina how she would feel if someone said that about her picture. *Wouldn't it hurt your feelings?* Marge asks. Christina allowed as how it would.

Marge tells me later, over lunch, that she wants the kids to be thinkers, be problem solvers. And I can see in Marge's teaching that she takes advantage of every opportunity to get the kids to sort things out, make inferences, draw conclusions.

Marge also never fails to create positive reinforcement for positive behaviors. *Thank you, Hamza, for raising your hand. Good job, Amaury. Thank you for sharing.* Marge never raises her voice. Never says "don't." And I'm impressed by the busy, industrious atmosphere of the class and by the orderliness of the 23 five-year-olds.

Natural Teacher, Natural Teaching

Marge, from Portsmouth, New Hampshire, with graduate work in developmental education at Northeastern University in Boston, knows to create opportunities for her children to read and write. She knows that not everything that needs to be learned must be explicitly taught. Marge knows to watch and celebrate what her children do, but she also knows that this doesn't mean a hands-off policy toward reading and writing. Rather, she knows, like Calkins (1994), that she must teach in response to what children do. Marge says she believes in "natural" teaching, in watching each child to see where and when she can facilitate the child's learning. She's "organic," she says, about participating in accordance to the individual learning path of each child.

Thoughtfulness

As part of the unit *All About Me*, Marge moves the kids back to the carpet for a critical thinking activity. The question is what kinds of pets the kids have. Marge draws a chart on the board, and from the kids' answers, she creates columns labeled *Dog, Cat, Turtle, Fish, Bird*, and *Other* (Fig. 5-4).

When Marge has listed all the pets the kids claim to have, she then polls each child individually. As the child locates where on the chart his or her pet should be accounted for, Marge darkens a box in the appropriate column.

After all the pets are accounted for, Marge asks, *Which pet do we have the most of? Next to the most?* Then, *Do we have more turtles than cats? More fish than turtles?* And so on. *Which pet do we have the least of?* Hicham wants to talk about his bird that died, but Marge manages to keep everyone on-task. Soon everyone seems to have the hang of "the most," "more than," and "the least."

In this simple activity, which flows organically out of the talking, reading, and writing that children are doing "all about themselves," they are cognitively engaged in classifying, evaluating, and analyzing "data." They are involved in creating a chart as a visual organizer of information and then generalizing from it for "findings" from their "research." These are some of the same behaviors that my university students need for success in *their* academic studies.

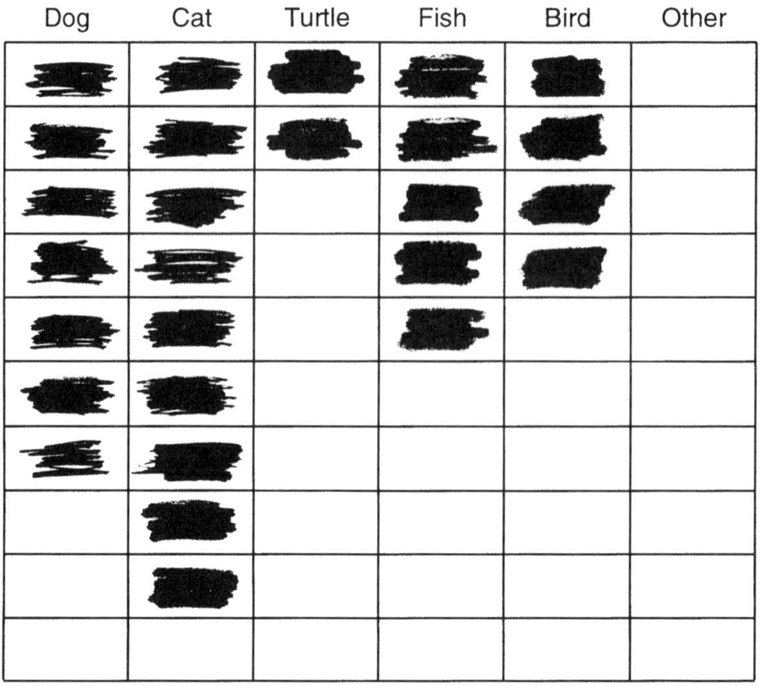

Dog	Cat	Turtle	Fish	Bird	Other
▬	▬	▬	▬	▬	
▬	▬	▬	▬	▬	
▬	▬		▬	▬	
▬	▬		▬	▬	
▬	▬		▬		
▬	▬				
▬	▬				
	▬				
	▬				

Figure 5-4   Pre-first graders do research; then they turn data into "findings."

◇◇ PRE-FIRST: *M*, NOCHA'S LETTER OF THE DAY

Name Game

Nocha's pre-first classroom is light, airy, and colorful, its walls covered with writing. To the side of the board, next to the reading carpet and low on the wall, is a chart reading "My name is _____." Below the chart is a large pocket holding as many cards as there are children in the class, each card printed with a child's name.

Once each morning and once again after lunch, a child picks his/her own name out of the pocket and affixes it on the line. ABCs run around the room. Pictures, shapes, and colors line the walls. Singing, led by Nocha playing the guitar, takes place on the "magic carpet" often each day. Today, they are singing "Special"—its lyrics on the big poster in front. Laila, Nocha's aide, follows along, moving her finger under the words as she sings with Nocha and the children.

The composition of Nocha's class is practically the mirror image of Marge's. Of Nocha's 23 mostly five-year-olds, only one (Damien) is a monolingual speaker of English. Three Indian sisters, triplets, speak English and other languages at home. One child, of American nationality, is bilingual in English and French. Fifteen of the children, of Moroccan or French nationality, speak Arabic or French, or Arabic *and* French at home. One child is a first-language speaker of Japanese. One is a first-language speaker of Spanish. And for one child, Rosanne—of Dutch nationality and a speaker of Dutch, German, and French—English is the fourth language.

Three of Nocha's students are brand-new to English, and to the school. The others entered the school in either nursery or kindergarten, which gives them one to two years already in English-medium schooling. Rosanne is brand-new to English—Nocha says she came in with "zero" English—and after one week, when the kids are gathering their lunch boxes for snacktime, Rosanne says, out of the clear blue sky, "My lunch box is on the school ground." Nocha, Laila, and I are dumbfounded, and very impressed. Yuji, the Japanese speaker, speaks little English, even though he has been in the school for a year. Maybe it's more accurate to say that Yuji, being a quiet child, simply speaks very little.

Even though Nocha and Laila speak only English to the children, the children speak multiple languages to each other. During collaborative work time, all common languages get brought into play by the children—whatever helps them accomplish their tasks.

Charades

After the song is over, Nocha moves to the big book *Things I Like*, one she has read before. Asking the kids what they remember, Nocha gets the response "painting." Nocha then acts out other activities, and the kids guess. Turning back to the book, Nocha turns the pages, asking the kids to find the activities she's acted out and they've guessed. Then, making expansive gestures of turning the pages, Nocha reads, gliding her finger along the words on the page.

As the kids listen and watch, Nocha asks them to tell her what actions begin with *m*, the letter of the day. Nocha is now standing at a giant chart that lists words like *mirror, me, mother, make,* and *more,* below a string of upper case *M*'s and lower case *m*'s. The kids then draw actions that start with *m*: *marching, mowing, melting,* and so on. Laila and Nocha move from child to child writing down what the child wants to say about the pictures.

Hesitation

Since the kids, without prompting, write their own names on their pictures, I wonder why they stop there. Why don't they let their writing tell the *rest* of the story that, perhaps, is not being fully told either through talk or drawing? Then it dawns on me that they think they don't know how to write. As I observe, I pick up subtle intimations that "they don't know how, because they haven't been 'taught' yet."

I feel torn. While knowing it is not my place to shape Nocha's teaching, I nevertheless feel that with the slightest encouragement the kids would be writing. When Nocha and I talk later, I ask about her plans for writing. Writing will come after the children "know" all their letters and letter–sound correspondences, she says. Like many teachers, Nocha seems tethered to a traditional sense of curriculum: The children will receive writing instruction later in the school year, and then they will be expected to write.

Yet, prompted by my question, Nocha says there is no real reason to wait—that's just "the way it's usually done." She says she'll be glad when the kids are not so dependent on her and Laila, as their scribes. Not realizing the restricting power of others' dicta over *her own* intuitions about literacy learning, Nocha lets others tell her what it means for her kids to "know." Yet, in regard to language learning, Nocha would not for a minute entertain the notion that her children don't know how to say that which they have not been explicitly taught. The contradiction doesn't occur to her.

Let Mrs. Myers Guess

Nocha gathers the children in a circle, whispering to Damien, the only monolingual English speaker in the class, to act out "picking apples." Laura, a home speaker of French, whose twin Alice is in Marge's pre-first class, guesses what Damien is doing. After Nocha whispers to her, Laura acts out "reading a book." And on it goes for a few minutes. I notice the ample language needed to accomplish these transactions, and the potential internalization of each notion. The activity is such fun that it's almost to be overlooked as a language "lesson."

Nocha shifts to the game of "Let Mrs. Myers Guess," the kids acting out actions for Nocha's benefit. She guesses correctly one child "thinking," then another child "flying," then "crawling," and so on. When one child does something related to a recently read story, *Whistle for Willie*, Nocha picks up the book and several children help her find the page. The children's classroom lives are lived in and out of the books they become increasingly familiar with, and whatever happens gets related back to something they have read. This is the budding of "intertextuality."

Bilingual, Bicultural Self

Nocha was born and raised in Canyon, New Mexico, in a large Spanish-speaking family in a close-knit mountain community. Her mother, Nocha says, was for some reason the member of the community everyone sought to help out at weddings, funerals, and other community occasions. Being the youngest child in the family and the only girl, Nocha always accompanied her mother. From her childhood, she remembers lots of weddings and funerals—and the ancient annual Catholic ritual of the *Hermanos Penitentes*, carrying crosses and crawling on their knees.

Although her community was close-knit, Nocha explains, and her family was very much involved in the social life of the community, something set her family apart. In a community where families had been Catholic for generations, since New Mexico was Mexico and belonged to Spain, Nocha's family was Protestant. Nocha has no idea how her family came to be Protestant, but grew up knowing that it was her mother's family, not her father's, who had converted long ago.

Nocha says she grew up with a sense of distinction between Hispanics and Indians in the Taos region, the two groups living in separate societies. Among Hispanics, she felt herself to be both an insider, because of her heritage and language, and an outsider, because of her family's religious "differentness." To function both inside and on the margins has been her way of life.

Upon finishing high school, Nocha was sent to a small Protestant college in southern Indiana. After graduation, she went to London to work for a publisher of religious books, where she met her husband, Dallas, who worked for the same company. She and her husband came to Morocco when he was hired by a foundation to organize projects for retired American executives who volunteer for overseas work in developing countries.

The mother of twin boys, also students at the school, Nocha is warm, gentle, and unassuming. By the end of the first week of the school year, the kids seem at ease with her and already clear about what is expected of them. When Nocha thinks the kids are getting noisy, and order needs to be restored, she rings a little brass bell, and the "ding ding" brings quiet to the room and focuses the children's attention. On this morning, between 9:20 and the lunch break at 11:55, she rings the bell twice. While structured, Nocha's instruction is not rigid or overly regimented, and all the children are engaged.

Naps, Music, and Art

After lunch, the kids rest on their mats, with soft, classical music playing in the background. And after rest, they go to the art room, where they draw one picture after another in response to directions given by Ana, their art teacher. *Draw a tree. Draw a flower. Draw a person . . . anybody you want . . . a brother, a sister, yourself. Draw a house. Add a sun and clouds to the picture of your house.* Ana, a young and perky Filipina, bounces about the room, praising the children's drawings.

At some point, Ana says she's going through her "checklist." *Do you have a tree? Hold it up! Do you have a flower?* And, in this natural way, Ana reinforces the vocabulary and keeps up the pace.

M and m's

Back in Nocha's room, the children pick out picture cards of things that "start" with the letter *m* —*mailbox, mirror, mop, motorbike, map*, and so on. Then they draw all the things they can think of that start with *m*. Kamal, a home speaker of Arabic and French, draws a *monkey, mask, moon, monster*, and some *milk* and *marbles*, along with a few *M*'s scattered around (Fig 5-5). Kamal then asks Nocha to label some of his figures, which she does.

Nocha then gets out the modeling clay, and the kids set out to mold into being something that starts with the letter *m*. Laura, a French speaker, leans over and whispers to me that she's making a monster. *Oooh, I'm afraid*, I say. Laura gloats. *Monster begins with M*, she says, with boastful certainty. Habiba, from a French/Arabic bilingual home, comes over to show me her clay. Catching me jotting notes in my journal, Habiba asks if I have any *m*'s. We search together and come up with several. She seems pleased. Clay mice, moons, mustaches, and monsters fill the room.

Trusting Intuition

Over lunch the next day, Nocha asks me for tips . . . asks if I've noticed anything she could be doing differently. Careful about crossing the line into evaluation and grateful for Nocha's openness in inviting me into her classroom "at any time," I say that I think

Figure 5-5   Kamal's "M" drawings: *monkey, moons, mask, marbles, monster, milk.* Labeled at Kamal's request by Nocha, his pre-first teacher.

she's wonderfully supportive of the children and creative with them. *No*, she insists, *Really, is there anything you can suggest? I'd be grateful.*

I tactfully suggest that she encourage the kids to write, and we talk a little about the concept of emergent literacy. One idea sparks another. With little urging from me, we agree that kids already have notions about literacy to act on and test out before "reading and writing" are "taught" in the school curriculum. That literacy manifests itself in nonconventional ways before kids' literate ways become more and more conventional. That, in drawing, kids are representing meaning, too, and young children move naturally and smoothly between drawing and writing. And that writing, talking, and drawing are simply different ways for children to represent and manifest their stories.

Nocha and I then talk about literacy as a linguistic process, with both internal and external dimensions. Literacy, as an internal process of forming hypotheses and testing them out as to how an (English) alphabetic system works. And as an external process involving social interaction that allows kids to appropriate words and print from their surroundings and experience what literate people do with written language.

At this point, I suggest that Nocha think of more functional uses for her students' writing and reading. And I promise to bring her copies of articles on emergent literacy by Early (1990), Hudelson (1986), and Sulzby (1985). Nocha seems relieved to have what she sees as "professional" encouragement for what she intuitively senses about the kids. In the weeks that follow, I see Nocha and her class increasingly engaged in literacy development.

◇ ESL PULL-OUT FOR FIRST GRADERS: EILEEN'S *BROWN BEAR* LESSON

Brown bear, brown bear, what do you see?
I see a purple cat
Looking at me.

Purple cat, purple cat, what do you see?
I see a white dog
Looking at me. . .

Brown Bears and Purple Cats

Radouan and Joudy, Arabic-speaking cousins from Syria, Anna from Poland, Luis from Spain, Edward from France, and Youssef, a Moroccan Arabic speaker, spend two hours with Eileen every morning, while their first grade classmates are doing "regular" language arts. Eileen is also doing language arts with her six charges, but with more focus on English-language fluency, since these children are all brand-new to English. Their first grade classmates, in two separate first grades, have all been at the Casablanca American School for several years now and are more fluent in English, so these six need extra attention in order to "catch up."

As the key player in this instructional design—involving Eloise and Patricia, the two first grade teachers, and Kim, the lower school principal—Eileen is the ESL specialist and all-around advocate for these children. Coordinating her lessons with Eloise and Patricia and pressing Kim for whatever materials and supplies she needs, Eileen makes sure that nobody falls through the cracks.

Primary Goal

Eileen's primary goal is to help these kids build a foundation as quickly as possible, so that they can fold back into their regular classroom language arts program as quickly as possible. To do this, she needs to get them to the point of being able to use the language of the classroom and its instructional apparatus as "comprehensible input" (Krashen, 1982). In other words, these kids need to quickly get to the point where they are not in over their heads—where they can function and perpetuate their own language and literacy development, with help, of course, from Patricia and Eloise, their first grade teachers.

Even with so much riding on Eileen's work with the kids, and with no time to spare, you would never know—to watch Eileen—that she and the kids were there to do other than have a good time. Cheerful, playful, perky, confident, and comfortable with herself, she makes the children feel they are special, wonderful, and *extreeeemly* bright. She is *soooo* lucky to get to work with them. And whenever they do some little something that they couldn't do even moments before, she is *verrrry* impressed. And she couldn't be prouder. The kids giggle, beam, and go on to their next accomplishment. And their language and literacy develop moment by moment.

Shapes and Colors

Eileen starts the "brown bear" lesson with vocabulary of shapes and colors, using flash cards and creating games to turn the lesson into play. Eileen turns *everything* into play. After the kids identify the colors of the cards, Eileen sends them scurrying about, searching for colors in the room. One child discovers "brown" on the cover of the big book Eileen has planted in the children's path, and she makes a big deal out of the discovery.

Figure 5-6 Eileen at work in her pull-out ESL class of first graders

Eileen then reads the big book *Brown Bear, Brown Bear, What Do You See?* the pages facing outward to the children, her finger following the words at the bottom of each page. The kids pick up the story structure readily, and start helping Eileen answer each question. Periodically she "forgets," and the kids jump in to supply the answer.

Eileen just *happens* to have all the animal shapes on paper sheets, which the kids color, consulting the big book for the appropriate colors as they work—*brown* bear, *red* bird, *yellow* duck, *purple* cat, *white* dog, and so on. After finishing their coloring, they cut out the animals and glue them to flat sticks to make puppets.

Physical Response

When the puppets are ready, Eileen chants the big book, setting the beat with snapping fingers. The kids match the stanza to the appropriately colored animal by holding up a stick puppet. *Purple cat, purple cat, what do you see?* chants Eileen. Anticipating the answer, the kids hurriedly set down their purple cats and raise their white dogs. Responding to Eileen's question, the kids chant in unison, *I see a white dog looking at me.*

Once the kids seem at ease with the vocabulary, Eileen has them use the puppets as "masks," holding them up in front of their faces and singing out the questions and responses. Red Bird asks Purple Cat, *Purple cat, purple cat, what do you see?* Purple Cat, looking over at White Dog, responds, *I see a white dog looking at me.* The kids soon have it down pat.

With Eileen prompting, the kids begin charting a slightly different course with *Teacher, teacher, **who** do you see?* And Eileen chants back, *I see children looking at me.* Next, with everyone seated, they go around the table, starting with Radouan, who's seated next to Joudy, who says *Joudy, Joudy, who do you see?* And Joudy chants back, *I see Radouan looking at me.* They continue until everyone has looked at everyone.

An enormous brown bear, a gift from the school's art teacher, hovers over this scene from the entrance wall. Starting below it, and filling up one side wall, are large sheets of butcher paper on which Eileen has printed the whole chant. *B* is the letter of the day, and, next, everyone's job is to find things in the classroom beginning with the sound /b/. Well, that's easy. Edward claims "bear," Joudy claims the "brown" of the bear, Youssef lays hands on "book," Luis finds "basket," Radouan locates a plastic "bucket" full of crayons, and Anna, remembering a "barking" dog in a book they read last week, scrambles to find the page. Eileen is verrrry proud.

And I am impressed, since three weeks prior to this day, the children knew no English, no English *at all.* As I marvel at the easy flow and organic feel of this "lesson," I am reminded of a statement by Vygotsky that . . . *teaching should be organized in such a way that reading and writing* [and, I would add, talking] *are necessary for something* (quoted by Britton, 1989, p. 217). To play a game, sing a song, complete a puzzle, stage a play . . . Eileen has the children talking, reading, and writing to some end. Then she raises the bar, so that the next "end" is more of a stretch, but, because her planning is flawless—and her intuitions well honed—the kids achieve it with ease, and with pride and joy.

∞ FIRST GRADE CLASS: PATRICIA'S CRITICAL DIALOGUING

Jobs to Do

In Patricia's class, everyone has a job to do. On the wall, there is a "turn-taking" wheel, with habitual jobs listed around its outer rim. On an inner wheel are the names of all the children in Patricia's first-grade class. The inner wheel is rotated every morning by the first child to enter the room, and each child then checks to see his or her job for the day. *Feed the fish. Water the plants. Straighten the books in the reading corner. Update the calendar*—by pulling the appropriate cards out of the pocket hanging below the wall calendar and affixing the day of the week, date, and weather (*sunny, cloudy, rainy, cold, warm, hot, dry,* or any combination).

Like all the classrooms at CAS, Patricia's first grade class is made up, almost exclusively, of nonnative English speakers. Of Patricia's 22 students, *one* speaks English at home. The other 21 are speakers of French, Arabic, Chinese, Hindi, Dutch, Polish, Spanish, and/or Flemish. Fifteen of the 21 students come from bilingual homes, where the languages are some combination of the above.

Today, the two students who have pulled office duty go off to take the day's attendance slip to the principal's office. One of the two (Luis, of Eileen's pull-out group) is brand-new to English and to the school. Luis heads off to the office with his classmate Ahmed, already in the school for two years, and an old-timer to English by now. *Come on, Luis, let's go*, says Ahmed, taking Luis's hand.

Spelling Words

Patricia dictates the spelling words of the day: *we, can, go, I, will, help, not, you.* Patricia encourages with *If you don't know all the letters, just write the ones for the sounds you "hear."* When the kids finish writing, she calls on various ones to come to the board and write one of the words. When it's Luis's turn, one kid says, *Luis can't do it. He'll have a chance just like everyone else,* Patricia responds. Luis marches resolutely to the board and writes a shaky *I*, as if to say, *So there.* Radouan, who is also brand-new to English, goes to the board and writes *not*. Patricia moves around the room, checking the kids' spelling and stamping a big rabbit on the perfect papers.

Journals

Kenza and El Mehdi have pulled journal detail, and they quickly work from the stack of journals on Patricia's desk, reading out the name on each journal as they find its owner. Following Patricia's directions, the students either make sentences incorporating their new spelling words, then amplifying their sentences with drawings, or, if they don't want to use the spelling words, Patricia tells them to write anything they want.

Steering an effective middle course between regimentation and chaos, Patricia reminds them to put a capital letter at the beginning of each sentence and, at the end, a period. *If you need a word and don't know how to write it, well, just try writing it your way, or tell me and I'll help,* Patricia says, encouraging the kids to act on their hunches. Not appropriating the kids' ideas or supplanting theirs with her own, Patricia says, *Tell me anything. Write what* you *want to say.*

On one board Patricia has listed some words from one of the books they've recently read, and some children glance to the board to look for a word they need for their writing. Some use the dictionaries scattered about the room.

Before the journals get stacked back on Patricia's desk, she and the kids discuss what they've written, why they chose to write what they did, and any difficulties they had in doing it. This is part of Patricia's strategy of helping the kids gain awareness of their own processes—of writing, reading, thinking—and awareness of the need to reflect on what they think and do.

Talking Math

After journal writing, Patricia starts the math lesson with a song that gets everyone moving and using their number cards:

> *Stand up, sit down, show me four.*
> *Point up, point down, show me five . . .*

After the number cards, Patricia hands out dominoes, and, per Patricia's instructions, the kids draw the dominoes in their math journals, visually turned in four different ways, and then translate what they see into Arabic numbers, written as addition problems.

After domino play, the kids gather on the carpet, where Patricia has called them to "talk math." They talk through the math problems, using words like *sum, add, equals,* and other terms mathematicians use. (See Fig. 5-7.)

Need for More Critical Dialoguing

After the school day is over, Patricia and I talk in her classroom over photographs of her oil paintings, recently exhibited at a gallery show in Casablanca. Patricia is talking about the need for parents to talk more with their children. While fiercely loved and protected, the children in her class don't experience enough critical dialogue with the adults in their lives, Patricia thinks. *Why do you suppose this? I wonder why that? What do you suppose caused this? How might this be different if we did X, or Y?*

At Parents' Back-to-School Night the following week, Patricia

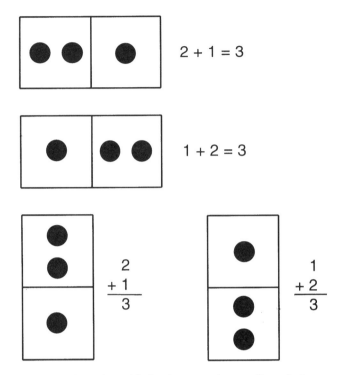

Figure 5-7 First graders play with dominoes as they "talk math."

plans to suggest diplomatically to the parents that they spend more time talking with their children. Patricia says she recalls one parent telling her that when the parent had asked her son about the similarity between candles and light bulbs, her child had answered "Both are yellow." And that had been the end of the dialogue. Patricia wants to approach the issue more systematically and with all the parents. Being French-Canadian and a fluent French-speaker herself, Patricia can easily handle the explaining she wants to do to the majority of her parents who may speak French, but not English.

At Parents' Night, Patricia plans to model asking questions. She also wants to encourage her parents to read together with their children, which she doesn't think they do. And, Patricia says, it doesn't matter what language they read in, since literacy proficiency transfers from one language to another. Patricia knows of the work of Jim Cummins (1984), and believes in his transference theory.

But, above all, Patricia worries about what she thinks is a lack of verbal engagement between the parents and their children. As Patricia and I close our conversation, I promise to bring her a copy of Shirley Heath's article, "A Lot of Talk About Nothing" (1991), which, I know, Patricia will find compatible with her sense of talk as central to learning, and to the development of critical thought.

◇◇ REFLECTIONS ON YOUNG CHILDREN'S LANGUAGE AND LITERACY LEARNING

In audio-taped sessions, as well as in subsequent written correspondence with Marge Gruzen, a pre-first teacher at the Casablanca American School, I asked Marge to reflect on her experience with young second-language speakers of English and their literacy and language learning. Her reflections are presented here in response to my questions.

◇◇ Q1: What thinking lies behind your lesson planning?

The language development of young second-language learners occurs best in an environment that incorporates the familiar with the unknown. To know where to start, I spend time observing the children to get a sense of how they think, respond, and react in language interactions. It is essential for me to read their body language and gestures while I listen to them talk.

After I determine their individual levels of proficiency, I can plan the curriculum to the specific language needs of the whole class—and the needs of each child. An integrated curriculum, encompassing all aspects of learning, is key to providing continuity and overlap of skills—and cognitive and linguistic development. When children are acquiring a new language, interaction and integration are central to their success. For language use to translate into language development, it needs a variety of situations, both real and imaginary.

◇◇ Q2: So how do you accomplish this integration and interaction in the classroom?

I plan thematic units. Thematic units provide a context for doing all sorts of interesting things. A unit of study that lends itself well to this approach is one I call *All About Me*. I designed the unit to promote body awareness, a sense of family, and self-esteem. I want to emphasize, though, that a unit cannot simply just be "plugged in." First, a teacher has to determine what a particular group of children needs—what they're ready for. Only then can an appropriate thematic unit be put in place.

Within a thematic unit, all disciplines become interrelated. Take, for instance, music, which is often isolated from language. Musical activities are wonderful for language development. Young children acquire language easily through rhythmic activities. Singing songs, with hand gestures that demonstrate actions, and physically moving and pointing to parts of the body—remember, as part of *All About Me*—and moving those *arms, legs, heads, hands,* and *fingers* to the words of the song, all make the learning of vocabulary easy.

My planning within the theme *All About Me* can be charted something like this:

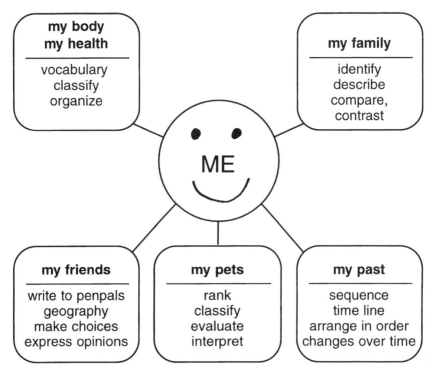

Figure 5-8   Integrating content for language and literacy development in a thematic unit, *All About Me*.

◇◇◇ ***Q3: I see the many possibilities for* All About Me. *It makes me think of the map of Early's "knowledge structures" (1990). What other units have you created?***

I like to start out with *All About Me*. Then I choose from these: *Dinosaurs, Weather/Seasons, the Solar System, Plants, Animals,* and *Celebrations*. My two favorite ones, ones the kids seem to like best, are *Dinosaurs* and the *Solar System*.

Whenever I know that a parent, or someone in the local community, has a special expertise in an area related to a theme, then, during the unit, I invite that person in to talk to the kids. Last year, when we were "in" the solar system, the father of one of the kids, who's an astronaut, came and gave a talk. The kids loved it.

We'll also plan field trips around a theme. When we did *Animals* last year, we visited the farm of a child in the class—a farm with cows, sheep, goats, chickens, and all.

⟨⟨⟩⟩ Q4: Could you map out another theme for me?

Let's do *the Solar System*. As with all new units, I would approach *the Solar System* with the children in this progression:

a. Question to the children: What do you already know?
b. Question to the children: What do you want to know?
c. Introduce new vocabulary (both general and specific) in the context of stories, pictures, videos, and manipulatives.
d. Read stories, sing songs, and teach poems that are all about the theme.
e. Engage the children in hands-on activities: puppets, moon rocks, drawing, reading, writing, videos, outside speakers, and so on.

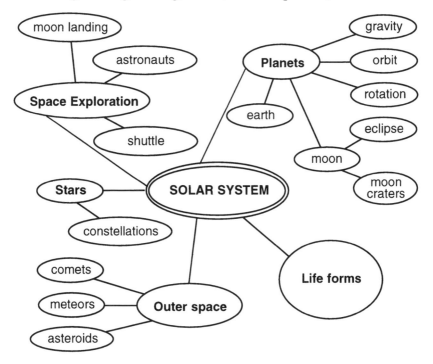

Figure 5-9   Integrating content for language and literacy development in a thematic unit, *The Solar System*

◇◇ Q5: Let's talk about writing. Where does writing fit into a unit?

We start out with drawing. Children love to draw. Drawing is how writing begins; drawing is visual representation of meaning, just as writing is. When given the opportunity, kids tend to choose familiar topics, such as themselves and their family, all a part of the unit *All About Me*. To assist in the development of language and literacy, I always label what a child draws in his own words. When the words are familiar, the child can read on his own and will retain and recycle those words more readily in future writings. So I begin with a language experience approach (LEA).

Labeling everything in the classroom, as to its English "name," is useful. I'm sure you've noticed the labels on everything in the room—*desk, chair, globe, map, toy box*, and so on. I see the children checking out those labels and incorporating the words into their writings.

During *All About Me*, the children keep a book about themselves, working on a different topic each day. The topics include anything about themselves, family members, what they were like as babies, their home, school, friends, hair/eye color, feet and hand prints, and so on. We clearly label the drawings, so the kids have those words for themselves. Children, from the beginning, need to be encouraged to write about what they draw, encouraged to move back and forth from drawing to writing in a natural flow. Their work is really "multimedia." They write–draw–talk.

Initially, the kids might say "I don't know how," but, when encouraged, they usually put down some representation. The kids "know," but sometimes they simply need the confidence to act on their "knowing." Or, their knowing is so internalized that it just needs to be brought to their awareness and expressed externally.

For me as a teacher, there is a parallel. At first, I had to reflect on my own sense of what children can do and act on that sense in my own teaching, just as I need to provide my kids with opportunities to act on their own sense of things. In the past, I would initially do all the kids' writing *for* them. I would write down everything they wanted said until I "taught" them the letters in some sort of formal, explicit way. But experience has shown me that children become dependent on the teacher, which makes for a more difficult transition to their own writing. When the teacher sends the message, even in subconscious ways, that kids can't write until taught by their teacher, then they internalize that message.

Any graphic representation, in the beginning, has some meaning to the individual child. Even before the formation of conventional letters, children are participating in the art of writing. When the vocabulary of writing is used—when, for example, the teacher talks to and about the kids as "writers," or I tell them to tell a story all the ways they want (drawing, writing, talking)—then they begin to develop an awareness of what they're doing and who/what they are expected to be.

Writing on a daily basis increases that awareness and provides an opportunity for teacher–student interaction, which soon develops into conferencing. Teaching the vocabulary of writing, such as "top of the page" or "under the picture," makes the transition into more accurate representation—into more conventional writing—a smoother process.

◇◇ Q6: What other lessons evolve out of a thematic unit?

Math, for one. Math concepts are grasped more readily when children are given manipulative materials they can touch, feel, and play with. They also grasp math concepts more readily when they are related to a framework they're already working in.

The tactile sense seems especially vital for second language learners. While handling materials, and modeling for the kids what to do with them, the teacher verbally labels for the children. When I use a variety of materials and recycle content and concepts, then I am reinforcing learning without reducing it to rote.

In the unit *All About Me*, activities such as counting body parts—arms, legs, heads—comparing and contrasting, measuring, solving simple word problems, both oral and written, require the use of similiar vocabulary, but in different settings. When math has meaning for a child, new concepts can then be transferred to other settings, other situations. Children can then use thinking strategies to use previously learned content. However, when only rote skills are taught as memorized bits, then kids have no mental agility with concepts, which, for them, serves more as information. It is difficult to transfer memorized information to other settings.

◇◇ Q7: We've talked about language, writing, and math. What have we forgotten?

Science and social studies. These areas of the curriculum play a big role in language development. Class discussions, role play, art/music integration, and writing tasks can be included. I can have kids doing brainstorming for topic selection, working on categories within topics, and classifying. Initially, brainstorming requires visual clues. I try to use the same visual clue for a word in all situations. The more written language becomes familiar to children, the more they succeed in incorporating it into their verbal and written activities.

Awareness of the world around them is in itself an important concept to grasp. I help them gain awareness by having them write/draw to pen pals in another country. Of course, this fits right into *All About Me*. Describing their lives to another child requires thinking and creative skills, as well as the development of more sophisticated expression.

◇◇ Q8: I'm surprised you haven't mentioned reading. Where does reading fit in?

Everywhere. Reading emerges, just as writing does. As with writing, I used to think kids couldn't do it until I "taught" them to. Of course, we still focus on reading, as part of kids' learning, but I understand it differently now.

In my experience with second language learners, teaching reading part to whole (phonics) is not really effective, if not taught in conjunction with whole to part teaching (whole language). Non-English-speaking children have a more difficult time taking unrelated parts and making sense out of them. Because of their lack of previous experience with English, they have little linguistic foundation to build on, of course.

Giving them the whole first, then focusing on one key area at a time, makes more sense for them. It certainly makes more sense *to* them! In the unit *All About Me*, choral reading of poems about themselves, families, and the world around them gives them the rhythm of language, similiar to music. Similarities of letters, words, and sentences can be then be pointed out and discussed.

I have discovered that *metalanguage*—language to talk about language—needs to be an integral part of an early childhood curriculum. When children understand the language of language, they can better use and retain information. Whole language activities, trade books, and poems lend themselves nicely to metalanguage training. We talk about words and what they mean, about how they look on the page, and how they feel in our mouths.

Having a child know the beginning and end of a sentence, what a sentence is made up of—my five-year-olds and I talk about that.

That's all part of metalanguage "talk." Then we work our way from there to words, syllables, and sounds. Talking about language—both written and oral—can only enhance a child's ability to understand more about language and literacy.

◇◇ Q9: So what advice would you give a new teacher who wants reading to develop within an integrated curriculum?

I would advise her to begin with the *whole*—that being a story or other complete text—and then systematically work from the whole to the parts within the whole. Phonics training can readily happen within this framework. As children become more curious about the spoken and written word, they will be listening for familiar sounds and will ask for information.

When a request comes from the kids, they are letting the teacher know they are ready for the information. *What about those little dots on the page?* one child might ask. Then I give them the name for a dot—a *period*—and we talk about sentences and how those little dots mark the boundary of a sentence. Discussions like this will show up in the kids' writing, as they gain more control over the details and "rules" of the written language.

◇◇ Q10: Kids have different learning styles and pace their learning differently. Plus, they're all at different points in their language and literacy development. How do you handle that?

These factors are a constant concern. True, children in pre-school function along a broad range of development. Opportunities for language acquisition must take this range into account. Classroom activities need to be open-ended whenever possible. Setting up work as "tasks" within a thematic unit allows children to work at varying levels: the less advanced child can grasp the basic concept or information being taught, while the more advanced child can move at a faster pace and possibly in different directions.

Trade books and sets of simple readers lend themselves well to themes. Books that fit into the theme-of-the-month provide more opportunities to read about familiar content. I'll collect all the books relating to the theme, put them out, and let kids follow their own interests, choose what they want. They browse and read. Also, I choose particular books to "fit" into a lesson. If I'm introducing a sound–letter pattern, I'll find storybooks with that emphasis.

◇◇ **Q11: What about the children's home time? Can you bring the parents in on integrating the children's learning?**

Even though the parents may not speak English, I send home a monthly calendar of home activities—written out in English—related to the theme we're working on/in at school. The children and I remind ourselves of the home activity of the day before they leave school, and we look at it on the board together.

Then, at home that evening, the children read the activity of the day to their parents. Do they really read it? Maybe yes, maybe no. Some of them may just remember what we said earlier at school. It is impossible to say when exactly any child moves from pretend-reading to actual-reading. But reading always starts with pretend-reading.

Here's the calendar I sent home when we started out the school year with *All About Me*:

Home Activities for September

Sunday	Monday	Tuesday	Wednesday	Thursday	Friday	Saturday
			1	2		3 Count as high as you can.
4 Find the letters of your name in a magazine or newspaper.	5 Share your favorite book with someone at home.	6 How many windows do you have in your house?	7 Make up a silly song ♬	8 Help set the dinner table.	9 Be nice to your teachers today ☺	10 Read a story to yourself.
11 Find 5 blue things in your room.	12 What kind of hair do the people in your family have?	13 Say your ABC's to someone at home.	14 Bring your telephone number to school.	15 Make the letter B, and use it to make a silly picture.	16 Try not to watch T.V. today. Play a game!	17 Draw a picture of your favorite thing to do.
18 Help clean up your room!	19 Find 5 things that are bigger than you.	20 Eat a healthy snack today.	21 Find out when your birthday is.	22 Read a book before you go to bed.	23 Count all the pets in your house.	24 Make up a new game today.
25 How many doors do you have in your house?	26 Sing a song to mommy or daddy.	27 Play with your teddy bear today.	28 Count the chairs in your house.	29 Count the different flowers in the garden.	30 Find 5 things that are smaller than you.	

Figure 5-10   Calendar of home activities for the unit *All About Me*

◇◇ **Q12: What problems are inherent in teaching a theme-based integrated curriculum?**

Having everything taught by the classroom teacher allows for the possibility of *truly* integrating everything. The topic of the day or week could be investigated in depth, throughout *all* the disciplines. The downside would be that the children would not have the opportunity to work with those truly capable "outside" specialists like Eileen [the ESL teacher].

So, the really ideal situation would be to have all adults come to the children, as Eileen does now. Time would be set aside within a school day, or at least in a school week, for the teaching team to meet and plan an integrated curriculum. As it is now, Eileen and I just *make* the time to integrate our work. The other areas, music and all, are simply not integrated at all.

Within a truly integrated curriculum, everyone involved would work as a team. Decisions would be made on how a language concept or skill would be taught. This way, there would be consistency throughout the day. I believe this approach would broaden the children's language and literacy development and meet all their cognitive, linguistic, and curricular needs more effectively.

◇◇ Q13: So, tell me, how do you see the overall framework for an integrated curriculum?

Remember that, almost to a student, my kids are not home speakers of English. They may hear and speak English *only* at school. (In some instances, the kids go home and teach their parents English.) So, I see language development as the primary and necessary focus in their curriculum. However, I do *not* see language development as a separate dimension involving a separate "lesson," with a specific time of day set aside for its teaching and learning.

Language development is a continuum that grows as the children grow. And it is clear that a second language, in all of its dimensions, takes many years to be acquired. English, as the medium of instruction here, does the work of fostering creative expression, critical thinking, and communication. It is the "whole" of the sum of the parts of learning. English-language development in my classroom is the umbrella under which all other aspects of learning take place. It is simultaneously the framework, the object, and the medium of learning and teaching.

All of my lesson planning, tasks, and activities must consider the children's level of English and the level they need to attain. Planning must be done accordingly. I'm always trying to teach to the level of the kids, while providing tasks and activities that will increase their level. And, remember, they're not all at the same level. So the tasks and activities have to provide the assistance—the scaffolding—that gets them to their next learning level. (See Cazden, 1982, for further explanation of *instructional scaffolding*.)

All areas of the curriculum need to be adjusted to meet the language needs of each child. The kids themselves are always the best measure a teacher has for knowing if the learning tasks are appropriate and achievable. A teacher watches her children and can "read" whether they grasp what's going on. How do I know? Well, having a child explain—in his own words—what we're doing: that helps. Another way is to have the child teach the lesson to another child. Listen and watch. Engage them in a conversation about it. You can know.

An important behavior a teacher can teach children is reflecting on what they know and don't know. They gain so much from this kind of awareness. Many second language learners, in my experience, have a difficult time even knowing that they don't know. They can go through an entire lesson, being sure they understand, and when the follow-up activity comes along, they're lost, although they don't know it. It took me a while to figure that out. I used to use up a lot of time reteaching what I had supposedly taught. And the freshness and excitement are gone if you have to redo a lesson. (This is different, mind you, from recycling concepts and vocabulary, which a teacher should do all the time.)

◇◇ Q14: Any more thoughts on language development?

You asked me earlier about advice for a new teacher teaching an integrated curriculum to ESL children. I'd want to talk to her about "survival" language for the classroom. It needs to include the vocabulary for asking questions during discussions. This is part of the metalanguage of the classroom. I always model question-asking for the children. Then we role-play it.

Classroom discussions are a great way for a teacher to know what her children know. When they interact with each other, children are displaying their language development spontaneously. In contrast, if children were asked to respond to rote questions, they would give back what they knew the teacher wanted to hear, not always knowing what they were responding to.

Listening to dialogue at the snack table or on the playground during recess is also a good way to gauge language development. Children often role-play during free time, and it is, many times, a conversation recycled from the classroom. If a child has been introduced to something new, he might attempt to use it during recess time.

I would want to reemphasize, to a new teacher, that language should not be taught in isolation. That is why an integrated curriculum is more successful—because nothing is taught in isolation. Pulling a child into a corner of the room, teaching him a skill, and then putting him back into the whole group to use that skill is not always effective teaching.

In a pull-out situation, you are teaching a small part of language that has little meaning in the child's world. Bits and pieces taught in isolation don't always transfer into new situations, new contexts. So, they're often useless. That's why pull-out ESL doesn't work unless it's coordinated with regular classroom instruction.

On the other hand, if that same "piece" is taught in the child's natural environment, she will then have more opportunities to use it, to really know it, in the familiar surroundings in which it was learned. This insight into my own teaching has been very important, very useful to me here in a multicultural, multilingual setting.

◇◇ *Q15: What do you see as your successes here, in this culturally and linguistically rich and complex teaching environment?*

Initially, some of the ESL children entering first grade were labeled as needing extra language help in the spring of their pre-first year. Then, the ESL specialists had the choice of pulling children out for special instruction; or they could choose not to label the specific children.

If the ESL specialists chose not to designate some children for special instruction, then they had to give the whole class extra time for language and literacy development. Basically, the choice was "pull out" or work "in-house."

In one pre-first classroom, a group of children were pulled out—well, actually pulled "aside" to a corner of the room—and given extra work on letter sounds, sound blending, and word recognition. In the other classroom—which happened to be mine—the ESL specialist (Eileen) worked with the classroom teacher (me) to provide more language opportunities. And she worked within the integrated curriculum that I had set in motion. In effect, we had an experiment in the making, although we hadn't planned it that way. We were simply trying to figure out the best way to help the kids.

Although there is no "formal" data to conclude *which* children developed more language and literacy—the ones pulled aside or the ones taught as part of the whole—I *know*, as the latter teacher, that, without a doubt, *all* my children benefited from the focus on language and literacy activities. At the age of five, some children might be truly ESL "candidates," while others are simply at a different developmental level. It is not always possible to tell.

Bringing the ESL specialist into the integrated curriculum I had set up gave another dimension to it. It allowed for skills previously taught to be practiced in a different format. And it gave a second adult a chance to interact with the children. Nothing can be lost and everything gained by having other teachers observe and co-teach with you. This gives you feedback on how and what the children are learning, and it gives you the opportunity to stand back, reflect, and become a better observer of the children. This gives you more opportunities to learn from them.

◇◇ **Q16: I know you were trained in special education. And, here you were, "forced" into being an ESL teacher, since no matter what you teach in a school like this, where almost everyone is a nonnative speaker of English, everyone has to "teach" ESL! So, what was it like, in the beginning?**

In the beginning, I found it *very* difficult to understand second-language learners and how they think. Coming from a special education background, all I had to go by was my training with language-impaired children. Of course, the learners here are not impaired, but I could still apply some of my training. It's just that the kids here respond much more quickly—learn more quickly—than those I had been trained to teach.

If I used visual clues and tactile input, along with oral language, I found the children here more attentive. I found they retained more than if I only spoke.

I also noticed that second-language learners need new content in smaller increments—to be able to absorb it and use it—than do first-language children. That seems obvious, but it was something I had to discover for myself. I then began chunking new content into more manageable amounts, *and* working harder at tying it to what they already knew.

I learned, of course, that literacy training is more successful if the developmental needs of the children are taken into account. This means that introducing something just because the curriculum requires it does not always benefit the children, not if they're not ready for it. An overemphasis on academics at the preschool level can result in canned programs with a lot of rote learning. The language in these programs is usually highly predictable, which means that the children learn to second-guess the material without really having to *think*.

With a curriculum rigidly prescribed, there isn't always room for spontaneous discussion or child-to-child interaction. It's always preferable—understatement of the year—to use materials with a high interest level, at the appropriate developmental level. It's important that the classroom teacher give her children every opportunity to use language interactively, and to leave room in the curriculum for interaction. This is what is meant by a "child-centered" curriculum.

◇◇ Q17: Any last reflections on your work with multilingual, multicultural children?

From my experience, here are the keys to success with second-language children:

◇ curricular consistency, as provided by an integrated, thematic curriculum;

◇ opportunities for kids to develop that tap into their considerable resources of curiosity, high energy, readiness to please others, and their pleasure in their own learning;

◇ teaching that taps all modalities of learning.

◆ REFERENCES

Britton, J. (1989). Writing-and-reading in the classroom. In A. H. Dyson (Ed.), *Collaboration through writing and reading: Exploring possibilities* (pp. 217–246). Urbana, IL: National Council of Teachers of English.

Calkins, L. C. (1994). *The art of teaching writing*. Portsmouth, NH: Heinemann.

Cazden, C. B. (1982). Adult assistance to language development: Scaffolds, models and direct instruction. In R. Parker & F. Davis (Eds.), *Developing literacy: Young children's use of language* (pp. 3–18). Newark, DE: International Reading Association.

Cummins, J. (1984). *Bilingualism and special education: Issues in assessment and pedagogy*. Clevedon, England: Multilingual Matters.

Early, M. (1990). Enabling first and second language learners in the classroom. *Language Arts, 67*, 567–575.

Heath, S. B. (1991). A lot of talk about nothing. In B. M. Power & R. Hubbard (Eds.), *Literacy in process* (pp. 79–87). Portsmouth, NH: Heinemann.

Hudelson, S. (1989a). "Teaching" English through content-area activities. In P. Rigg & V. G. Allen (Eds.), *When they don't all speak English: Integrating the ESL student into the regular classroom* (pp. 139–151). Urbana, IL: National Council of Teachers of English.

Krashen, S. (1982). *Principles and practice in second language acquisition.* New York: Pergamon Press.

Sulzby, E. (1985). Kindergartners as writers and readers. In M. Farr (Ed.), *Advances in writing research, volume one: Children's early writing development* (pp. 127–199). Norwood, NJ: Ablex.

◆ RELATED REFERENCES: FOR FURTHER READING

Au, K. H. (1993). *Literacy instruction in multicultural settings.* Orlando, FL: Harcourt Brace Jovanovich.

Collier, V. (1987). Age and rate of acquisition of second language for academic purposes. *TESOL Quarterly, 21*, 617–641.

Collier, V. (1992). A synthesis of studies examining long-term language-minority student data on academic achievement. *Bilingual Research Journal 16* (1 & 2): 187–212.

Dyson, A. H. (1983). The role of language in early writing processes. *Research in the Teaching of English, 17*, 1–30.

Early, M., Mohan, B., & Hooper, H. (1989). The Vancouver school board language and content project. In J. H. Esling (Ed.), *Multicultural education and policy: ESL in the 1990s* (pp. 107–124). Toronto, Canada: O.I.S.E. Press.

Freeman, D. E., & Freeman, Y. (1994). *Between worlds: Access to second language acquisition.* Portsmouth, NH: Heinemann.

Heath, S. B. (1982). Ethnography in education: Defining the essentials. In P. Gilmore & A. A. Glatthorn (Eds.), *Children in and out of school: Ethnography and education* (pp. 33–55). Washington, DC: Center for Applied Linguistics.

Moll, L., & Diaz, R. (1987). Teaching writing as communication: The uses of ethnographic findings in classroom practice. In D. Bloome (Ed.), *Literacy and schooling* (pp. 195–221). Norwood, NJ: Ablex.

Teale W. H. & Sulzby, E. (Eds.). (1986). *Emergent literacy: Writing and reading.* Norwood, NJ: Ablex.

Wong Fillmore, L. (1989). Teaching English through content: Instructional reform in programs for language minority students. In J. H. Esling (Ed.), *Multicultural education and policy: ESL in the 1990s* (pp. 125–143). Toronto, Canada: O.I.S.E. Press.

◆ THOUGHT STARTERS
for reflection, journal writing, and/or discussion:

1. Consider the role of journals in language/literacy development. How can young children or children new to English use journals? Why do Marge and Patricia use journals and not just sheets of paper?

2. Consider whether an integrated curriculum would work in high school. What difficulties would arise? Implications for ESL pull-out? Are themes the only way to integrate a curriculum? How does integration avoid rote learning?

3. Teachers might worry that "organic" teaching—following the child's lead—uses up too much time. How can a teacher balance child-centered teaching with effective time management?

4. How do "real and imaginary" purposes and audiences for speaking help translate language *use* into language *development*? How does the concept apply to literacy use?

◆ PROJECT STARTERS
for writing and research:

1. Individually or with others, develop a thematic unit of study (any level) patterned after *All About You*. Integrate as many language/literacy activities as seem appropriate. Be creative.

2. Pull-out programs are commonplace in ESL instruction. Read three journal articles on the subject and discuss your findings.

3. Review two to three articles on whole language. Specifically, read to understand the whole language/phonics debate. Summarize your findings and apply them to teaching.

4. Research Cummins's transference theory on literacy skills from L1 to L2. Relate your understanding and discuss implications for ESL teaching.

Chapter Six

"I Know Because I'm Big": Children Becoming Writers and Readers

'To know' means having been able to construct some conceptualization that accounts for a certain set of objects or phenomena within a given context of reality. Whether this 'knowing' coincides with socially accepted knowledge is another problem (even though this is precisely what schools consider to be *the* problem of 'knowing'). One child may know the names of letters (or conventional spelling) without understanding very much about the writing system. Conversely, another child may make substantial progress in understanding the system as such without ever having received any information about spelling.

—Emilia Ferreiro,
Literacy Acquisition and the Representation of Language

LIKE A BIRD

Zayneb, blondish brown ringlets crowning her tiny face, finds her seat at one of the octagonal tables in Ghizlane's kindergarten class. Four years old and a home speaker of Moroccan Arabic and French, Zayneb has been at the Casablanca American School (CAS) for a year—having entered at the nursery level—and already she uses English with ease.

The first one in from recess, Zayneb begins arranging the modeling clay in front of her, as I make eye contact and ask, with a twinkle in my eye, why she's chosen that particular spot to sit. *Because this is my seat*, she says with authority. *How do you know it's your seat*, I ask. *Because that's my name*, she says, pointing to the printed letters on the card taped to the table in front of her.

Pushing my luck, I ask Zayneb how she knows it's her name. Patient with my persistence, she runs her finger along the letters and says, *Because it says Zay-neb.* I press on. *How do you know it says Zay-neb?* I ask. Proudly puffing out her chest, like a little bird, she says with finality, *I know because I'm big.*

Aware that literacy is a large undertaking even for children who become readers and writers of the language of their home and surrounding community, I am at CAS to experience classrooms where children like Zayneb are becoming literate in a language that is neither spoken at home nor in their lives outside of school. For these children, literacy is an *enormous* undertaking.

In effect, the "first" literacy of these children is achieved in their second, or at least their "non-first," language, since they are too young to have been schooled in their home language(s). (This phenomenon I will refer to as *second language literacy.*) To make the learning situation even more complex, the children may not always have gained full fluency in speaking *in* English before they need to be well on their way to becoming writers and readers *of* English.

Over the weeks I spend with the children, in two kindergarten and two pre-first classes of mostly four- and five-year-olds, I become convinced that confidence in themselves as language and literacy learners, a confidence engendered by teachers and parents, is a key to their success. I get to know these children, who, like Zayneb, know because they're big.

OPERATING ASSUMPTIONS ABOUT LANGUAGE ACQUISITION

To review why I am with the children: I am interested in learning what accounts for successful second language learning but, more so, what accounts for successful second-language *literacy* learning. As I inventory my operating assumptions in order to make better sense of this new experience, I am aware of the following.

I know from experience—as parent to my own child, as *auntie* and friend to others' children, and as a reader of the literature—that very young children blossom into first language, over time, in a nurturing, interactive environment. The context, the environment, is *all*, and the central players—in addition to the children—are caring adults. Importantly, the caring adults act in ways that continuously and verbally engage the children. And these engagements serve a multitude of functions: display affection, relate, transact the business at hand, explain, attend to wants and needs, entertain, and mentor.

I know, we all do, that a caring adult in a young child's life conducts both interlocutors' roles in a conversation—holding up both ends—well before the young child utters anything remotely comprehensible. That, through a process of approximation and accommodation, the young child's utterances grow increasingly comprehensible to others.

In summary, my underlying assumptions about first language development are these: "language-getting" is an acquisition process, which, for a young child,

a. happens over time,
b. happens in stages or phases,
c. varies from child to child, in terms of its "time table,"
d. is characterized by continuous interaction and engagement by those who have already "got" the language,
e. is not altered by correction or formal instruction, and
f. is marked, and even driven, by "error."

By "error," I mean bits of unconventional child language resulting from the child's evolving hypotheses about the system (*two foots*, *goed home*, *ball* for anything round). "Errors" of this sort drive development in that they are a child's "trial balloons." Error forms get adjusted through feedback, usually in the form of modeling, which provides the input necessary *for* adjustment and modification. Perhaps the most awesome idea of all is that, ultimately, every child *constructs* a first language—or, in the case of a truly bilingual child, several first languages—from the bits and pieces she/he takes in. [Yule, 1996, pp. 175–189, provides a clear summary of recent research in child (first) language acquisition.]

OPERATING ASSUMPTIONS ABOUT SECOND LANGUAGE ACQUISITION

From prior personal and professional experience with second-language children, I know that when children are very young, the second-language "getting" process has much in common with the first. And school programs designed primarily to promote second-language development need to simulate, as much as possible, the interactive, nurturing environment that so effectively facilitates first-language growth.

At the Casablanca American School, three-year-olds in the half-day nursery program become English speakers through structured play with their peers, guided by English-speaking teachers. Play involves roles (e.g., in cooking, playing house), which in turn require language—names of things, polite commands, requests, and commentary. Role play extends into songs, games, drawing, coloring, and story time. Each cycle of action and interaction builds on another.

In such a language rich environment, very young second-language children blossom into language—in this case, into English. As with the first language, the second language

a. emerges over time,

b. emerges in phases or stages,

c. varies from child to child, in terms of its rate of development, and,

d. through a process of adjustment and readjustment on the child's part, becomes increasingly conventional and "correct."

As with a first language, the second-language process with young children

a. is characterized by intensive interaction and engagement by and with those who already "have" the language, who adjust their language use to a level the child can grasp, upping the ante as the child's proficiency increases;

b. focuses on real meaning—on language used purposefully to achieve some end—and does not focus, except perhaps momentarily, on form;

c. is not altered by correction or formal instruction; and

d. is marked and even driven by "errors," which result from children trying out bits of language and then, according to the feedback they receive, adjusting their hypotheses about the way the system works.

(Freeman & Freeman, 1992 [pp. 11–37] and 1994 [pp. 81–107], give clear and comprehensive overviews of second-language acquisition research, with particular reference to Cummins [1984] and Krashen [1982].)

In the weeks I spend in the nursery, kindergarten, and pre-first classes at the Casablanca American School, I see nothing that contradicts my assumptions about language acquisition. In fact, the growth of these young children reinforces everything I think to be true about young second-language children and the environments that best foster their language development.

QUESTIONS ABOUT LITERACY ACQUISITION

I come to this aspect of my study—learning about young children's second-language literacy development—prepared to see parallels between the processes of language acquisition and literacy acquisition, but I do not know how far the analogy between *emerging language* and *emerging literacy* will take me.

With nothing to "prove" and much to learn, I start off with two very simple questions, as I sit amid four- and five-year-old children, busy at work in kindergarten and pre-first classrooms. My questions are these:

1. *What is going on here?*
2. *How to explain the children's progress in acquiring literacy?*

The second question presumes that the children are, in fact, acquiring literacy. And even casual observation would say that that is so. Not surprisingly, I see children, even those new to English, learning literacy by being actively engaged in literacy activities, literacy events. As they listen to stories and are read to, as they respond to stories through drawing and spontaneous or encouraged writing, they are learning literacy.

The pre-first kids in particular, for whom literacy is more overtly an end-of-the-year instructional goal, increasingly "act" literate. That is, they begin to behave in ways that are more profound than simply producing writing that is increasingly conventional. One child might seek out a select book during free time or ask for a certain word she wants to spell "just right." As literacy begins to permeate their lives, certain turns of mind grow evident. One child comments on a story rather than telling it; another child establishes a perspective on one story by commenting on its difference from another story.

But I'm getting ahead of myself. I want to look microscopically at what is going on with the children, and then zero in on the critical factors that explain their progress in acquiring literacy.

WHAT IS GOING ON HERE?

Four pre-first grade children will help me illustrate what is going on. And, in choosing these four, my reasons are basically pragmatic: I have an abundance of their work, fairly evenly spread over the whole of the school year; and, since these four seem to prefer dark colors in their choice of markers and crayons, their work produces better copies. Anyone who has tried to duplicate children's work done in crayon knows the problem. Even with these four, in instances where the copies needed enhancement, I have carefully traced with dark ink, with great regard for the authenticity of substance and character of the original.

The children are these:

Child: Vincent
Home language: French
Grade: pre-first
Age at start of pre-first grade: five years old
Length of time in English immersion by start of pre-first grade: one year (enrolled at CAS in kindergarten)

Child: Hicham
Home languages: French and Arabic
Grade: pre-first
Age at start of pre-first grade: four and a half years old
Length of time in English immersion by start of pre-first grade: one year (enrolled at CAS in kindergarten)

Child: Claude
Home language: French
Grade: pre-first
Age at start of pre-first grade: five years old.
Length of time in English immersion by start of pre-first grade: two years (enrolled at CAS in nursery)

Child: Mira
Home languages: French, Arabic, and English
Grade: pre-first
Age at start of pre-first grade: five years old
Length of time in English immersion by start of pre-first grade: one year (enrolled at CAS in kindergarten)

Like a child whose literacy is newly emerging, I too want my (the children's) illustrations to occupy the fore. My words are secondary, here to support and enhance the illustrations, and not the other way around. As with hypertext, readers can now shift to the illustrations (pages 111-133) and study them for themselves, with the commentary attached to each as guide, and then return to the discussion below.

THE CHILDREN TELL US WHAT'S GOING ON: LOOKING AT THE WORK OF VINCENT, HICHAM, CLAUDE, AND MIRA

Despite the difficulty of becoming literate in a language different from your first language, or, in Mira's case, in a language that is only one of your first three languages, Vincent, Hicham, Claude, and Mira (and their classmates) are clearly engaged in successful literacy learning. (I won't quibble with those who might argue that Mira's case is a bit different from Vincent, Hicham, and Claude's, all three of whom use English only at school.)

Broadly stated, these children's literacy learning is taking place in a context where they are actively engaged in literacy events: They listen to stories, tell their own stories, spend time with books they select during free time, discuss what is read to them, and are encouraged to tell their own stories through drawing/writing. The children's work is treated with respect: The adults with them accept their drawing/writing to say whatever the children say it says, and invented spelling is not shunned or disregarded.

From these positive literacy experiences, Vincent, Hicham, Claude, and Mira have the support they need to test out their hypotheses about the way the written language system works and how literate people use written symbols to construct and represent meaning.

Even children like Vincent, Hicham, and Claude, who are only one year into English, and others who are even less fluent than they, can create meaning using all the available resources of the supportive classroom context that surrounds them. These resources consist of many sorts: labels all over the classroom, words related to the subject at hand on the board, books at their fingertips, two helping adults (a teacher and an aide), and a myriad of visual aids.

By examining samples of the work of the four, work they accomplish between September and April of their pre-first grade year, we can figure out what's happening (on page 134).

Figure 6-1
Date: 9/94. **Prompt:** Tell about the day you were born.
Vincent's reading: *You hoo, my mommy said. After, my daddy said. After, mommy said, Daddy, come see.*
Observation: Vincent recyles eight letters, four from his own name, to secure his narrative. Note the use of space and a dot to cluster the letters.

Figure 6-2
Date: 10/94. **Prompt:** In your journal, tell about something.
Vincent's reading: *I play with the puppet.*
Observation: Vincent's clusters, separated by dots, correspond more or less to syllables. For example, note Vincent's rendering of "PO·PXOA·" (puppet) as two clusters.

Figure 6-3
Date: 11/94. **Prompt:** In your journal, tell about something.
Vincent's reading: *Vincent is playing with the car,* as told to Zhor, the pre-first aide.
Observation: Vincent's clusters, still marked by dots, are beginning to correspond more to words: note "•PAICI•" for *playing.*

Figure 6-4
Date: 12/94. **Prompt:** In your journal, tell about something.
Vincent's reading: *This is Santa Claus coming,* as told to Marge, his teacher.
Observation: Perhaps he's actually written **Is Santa Claus coming?** Note his discovery of question marks. Vincent continues to use dots and blank space to cluster his letters.

Figure 6-5
Date: 3/95.
Prompt: Make a valentine and send a message.
Vincent's reading: *I love you, Valentine. Boo! Love, Vincent. Happy Valentine!*
Observation: Vincent's writing is now longer and more complex. Some of his clustering is hard to figure out, but words like "BOO" and "HAPPY" are clear. "UN" must represent *you* or *love*, and "V," *valentine.*

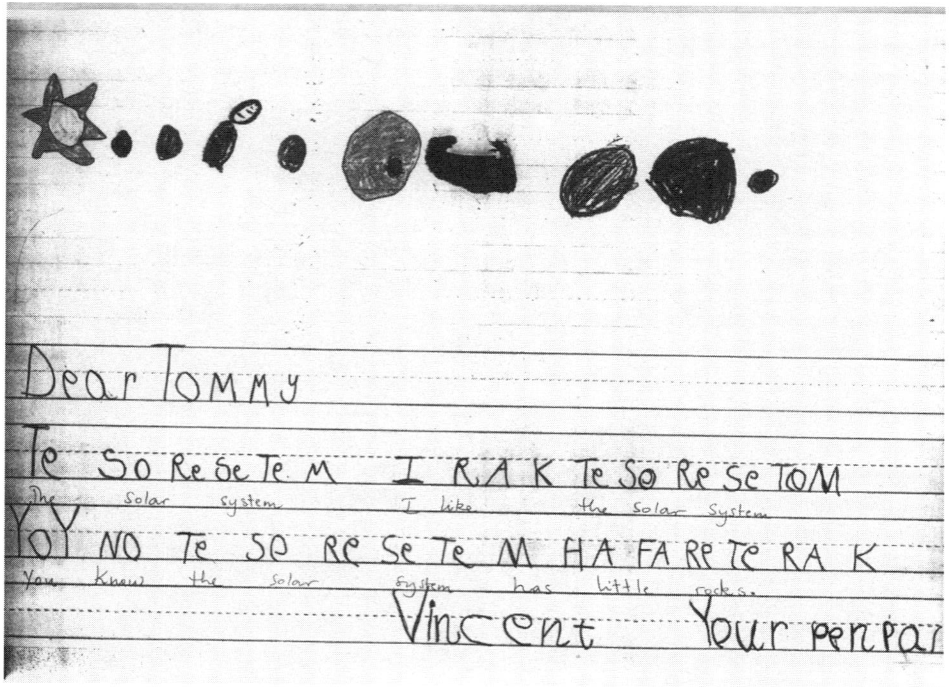

Figure 6-6
Date: 4/95.
Prompt: Write a letter to your pen pal.
Vincent's reading: *The solar system. I like the solar system. You know the solar system has little rocks.*
Observation: Since the class is studying the solar system, Vincent takes advantage. Note that he is actually conveying opinion and information through writing, not simply labeling his drawing, as he seems to do in his earlier work.

Dear TOMMY
Te So Re Se Te M I RAK Te So Re Se TOM
The solar system   I like   the Solar System
YOY NO Te SO Re Se Te M HA FA RR Te RA K
You know the solar   system   has   little   rocks
Vincent   Your penpal

Figure 6-7 Prompt: Tell about the day you were born.

Hicham's reading: Hicham says he doesn't know what it says.

Observation: To hold a place for a future message, Hicham is probably recycling the letters of his name as he writes "ICihHAEF." Six of the eight letters he uses are in "Hicham."

Figure 6-8
Date: 11/94. **Prompt:** In your journal, tell about something.
Hicham's reading: *One day, I saw a cat with me.*
Observation: Emergence of letter–syllable correspondence: each letter represents a separate syllable-word, except for "CT," *cat.*

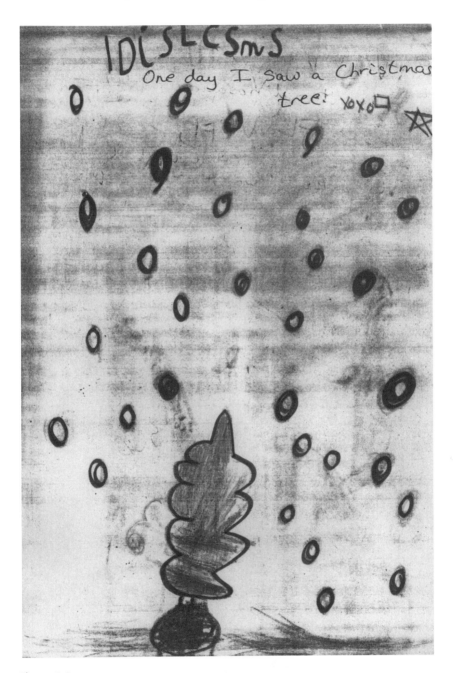

Figure 6-9
Date: 12/94. **Prompt:** In your journal, tell about something.
Hicham's reading: *One day, I saw a Christmas tree.*
Observation: Rather than simply one letter/one (syllable) word, a longer word now "needs" more letters: note "CSmS," for *Christmas.*

Figure 6-10
Date: 2/95.
Prompt: Make a valentine and send a message.
Hicham's reading:
Happy Valentine's Day!
Observation: Hicham continues working out the relationship between letters and speech. Although still focused on syllables, he shows increasing awareness of consonant sounds–symbols that begin or end syllables: note "HP," *happy;* "VLTM," *valentime;* "D Z/S," *days.*

Figure 6-11
Date: 3/95. **Prompt:** In your journal, tell about something.
Hicham's reading: *One day, Peter woke up to eat him his supper.*
Observation: Longer, more complex writing. Evidence of revision: note crossed-out letters as Hicham attempts *Peter* and ends up with "PDR." Some evidence here of sound–letter correspondence even to vowel sounds, as in "aP" for *up.*

Figure 6-12
Date: 4/95. **Prompt:** In your journal, tell about something.
Hicham's reading: *One day, the prince wanted to pick a flower for the queen.*
Observation: New use of space and dots to cluster letters. More revision: note "KWCN," becomes "KWN," *queen*. Evidence of complex sense of English directionality: note double line of writing, with second line also from left to right.

Figure 6-13

Date: 4/95.

Prompt: Write a letter to your pen pal.

Hicham's reading: *Dear Brian S. One day, I saw a superman.*

Observation: More conventional use of space and punctuation. Awareness of audience: Note that Hicham's information serves to communicate information to his reader, not just label or explain his drawing.

Figure 6-14
Date: 9/94. **Prompt:** Tell about the day you were born.
Claude's reading: Claude has nothing to say.
Observation: Unwilling to venture a written narrative, Claude places his name to the top left to claim ownership of the drawing; to the bottom right, he names the figure representing himself, although he also looks to be still *in utero*.

Figure 6-15
Date: 10/94. **Prompt:** In your journal, tell about something.
Claude's reading: *One day, I swam in a pool.*
Observation: Now Claude ventures to represent his narrative in conventional letters, although only "POL," *pool,* matches a somewhat conventional correspondence.

Figure 6-16
Date: 12/94. **Prompt:** In your journal, tell about something.
Claude's reading: *I like Apatasauras (?). He has a long neck. He eats plants.*
Observation: A conventional sound–letter correspondence is emerging: note the near completeness of "HEETPLS," *he eats plants.* Evidence of revision: note the second letter of "APTSORES" is crossed out, and then left in. (Claude's "research" undoubtedly results from the class unit on dinosaurs.)

Figure 6-17
Date: 2/95.
Prompt: Make a valentine and send a message.
Claude's reading:
Valentine is come on February 14, and on 14 February we gave hearts to someone.
Observation: Note the increasing length of what Claude is willing to venture. As in Figure 6-16, the directionality is complex: multiple lines, all reading left to right. Claude might be experimenting with appearance: note a capital letter to start each line and more cursive-like letters.

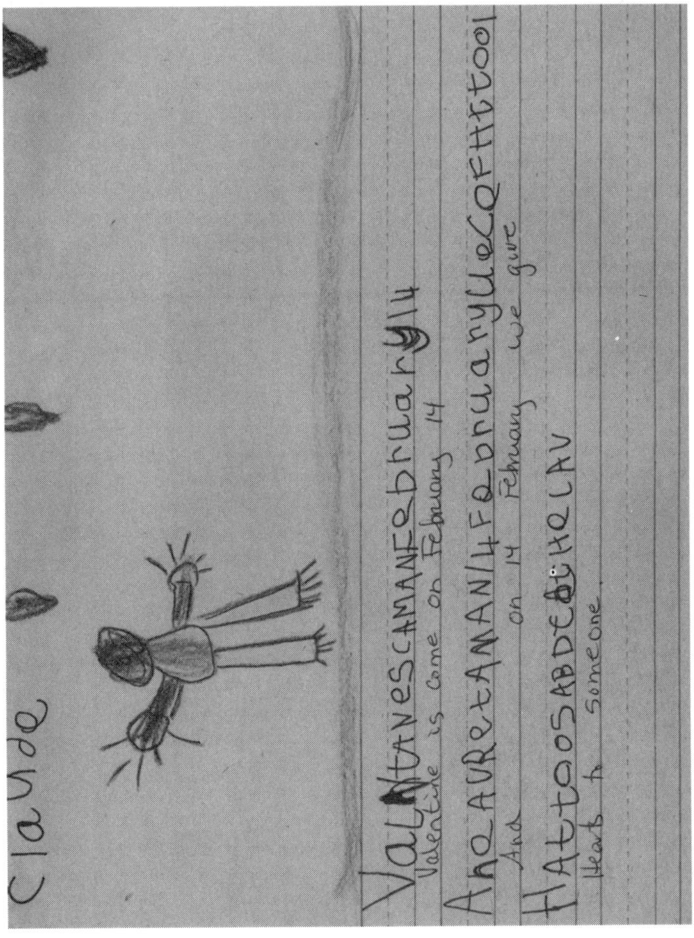

Figure 6-18
Date: 3/95. **Prompt:** Tell me what you like about the story *Mooncakes*.
Claude's reading: *I like it when the bear went to do [paint] the rocketship. 10–9–8–7–6–5–4–3–2–1, Blast.*
Observation: Claude's reading tumbles ahead of his writing: he's left out *when the bear went*. New use of space to cluster letters. Now a sense of literacy as serving multiple functions: both to express his opinion as well as label his drawing. Note that Claude's opinion ("I like . . .) occupies the visual center of the space, while he relegates his labeling of the drawing to a lower, off center, and smaller space.

Figure 6-19
Date: 4/95.
Prompt: Write a letter to your pen pal.
Claude's reading: *We are studying about space.*
Observation: Increasing use of space to cluster letters, as words. Greater use of upper case vs. lower case letters. Increasing sense of audience: note Claude's addition of his last name to communicate with someone unfamiliar. Clear sense that the drawing illustrates the writing, not the other way around.

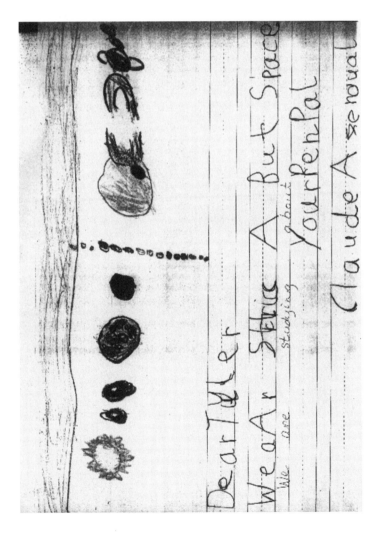

Figure 6-20
Date: 10/94. **Prompt:** In your journal, tell about something.
Mira's reading: *One day, I saw a little girl walking with her dog.*
Observation: Mira began pre-first grade already aware of "writing words" (cf. Figure 5-2, Chapter 5). Her journal entry displays a strong sense of sound–letter correspondence. Note, though, that her actual writing isn't keeping up with her more well-developed verbal intentions.

Figure 6-21
Date: 12/94. **Prompt:** In your journal, tell about something.
Mira's reading: *One day, I saw a Christmas tree in the woods.*
Observation: This more closely matches Mira's stated intentions. Note Mira's sense that longer words need more letters: "C-RECH–E/LMCH," *Christmas.* Note also Mira's well-developed sense of conventional directionality: for five lines, her writing reads left to right.

Figure 6-22. Prompt: Tell me what you like about the story *Mooncakes*.
Mira's reading: *I like it because it's funny.*
Observation: Because of the nature of the prompt, Mira foregrounds her writing, which is the expression of her opinion. The drawing is secondary, amplifying her writing. This is "mature" literate behavior. Note Mira's awareness of the need to revise, as evident in her writing from the start of the school year (Figure 5-2). She is also now using space to cluster her letters/words.

Figure 6-23
Date: 4/95.
Prompt: Write a letter to your pen pal.
Mira's reading: *One day, my mommy saw a guard peeing. My mommy laughed. The guard cried, and it was at a hotel.*
Observation: Whew, what a long, complex story! Note Mira's use of space and punctuation to approximate conventionality. Increasing use of upper case vs. lower case letters. New awareness of audience: note the numbers and arrows to direct her reader's view. Greater degree of revision: Mira went back and added "A GRD PEEN. My MyMM. LaFT" afterwards.

◇ Literacy learning is an emergent process. By that I mean that the reading and writing behaviors of young children develop *into* conventional reading and writing (Teale & Sulzby, 1986). In the writing of "my" four children, the sound–symbol correspondence becomes increasingly conventional. (The term "emergent literacy," connoting development rather than stasis, was probably first used by Clay, 1966, in her doctoral research, according to Teale & Sulzby, p. xviii.)

◇ As the children's literacy emerges, they pass through generally discernible, but not invariable, phases in figuring out the writing system. (Ferreiro & Teberosky, 1982, discern five stages, roughly comparable to those below, but literacy involves much more than mastery of the writing system.)

1. The lines and circles of an earlier stage (which I see in the writing of concurrently enrolled kindergarteners) give way to letters and letterlike forms. All four children's first writings of the school year display more letters than letterlike forms.

2. Directionality emerges. This is the way written symbols are turned (*d* vs. *b*) and, more profoundly, the direction of flow of a letter-stream, with the writer of English returning to the left to begin subsequent streams. In the writing of the four children here the direction of letter flow is already conventional, but we can assume that at some recent time, before the beginning of the current study, their writing was not conventionally directed, much like the writing of one of the concurrently enrolled kindergartners:

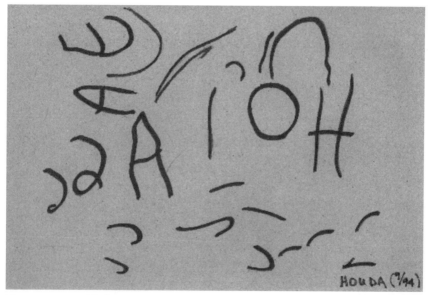

Figure 6-24 A kindergartner writes her name, "Houda." Compare Vincent's, Hicham's, Claude's, and Mira's well-developed sense of conventional (English language) directionality to Houda's.

3. One letter begins to correspond more or less to one syllable. Hicham writes *one day I saw* variously as "IDES" and "IDIS." As the children begin writing multisyllabic words, they realize they need to use more letters. For example, Claude writes *rocket*, "RCT." Hicham writes *Christmas*, "CSmS."

4. Either before or after letters begin to correspond to syllables, blank space (to cluster letters as words or wordlike forms) and punctuation begin to appear. Vincent, for example, figures this out *before* he uses letter symbols to represent sound, using both blank space and punctuation. Mira doesn't figure it out until *after* beginning to use letters to represent more than syllables—to represent seemingly discrete sounds.

5. As the children begin shifting away from operating by a (more or less) letter–syllable hypothesis, their letters become more *alphabetic* (representing individual sounds, not syllables). As they shift, consonant sound representations emerge first, and consonants get represented more consistently than vowel sounds. (This is not surprising since consonant sounds, produced by obstructing air, *seem* more discrete.) Hicham, for example, writes *Peter*, "PDR"; Claude writes *plants*, "PLS."

◇ Regardless of phase, children's literacy learning is influenced by story experiences, in activities that spin off of stories, as well as in thinking–writing in story narrative. For example, the kids' writings here often begin with *one day*, which is almost as stylized a story starter as *once upon a time*.

◇ Varying literacy experiences help young writers develop a sense of audience. In turn, a sense of audience influences a writer's behavior. The pen pal letters here show their writers' efforts in "connecting the dots" for unfamiliar readers. For instance, Vincent announces the "topic" of his letter ("Te So Re Se Te M"), before he discusses it. In signing his pen pal letter, Claude writes his full name, which he never does on work for his (familiar) classmates and teacher.

◇ As the kids grow increasingly literate, the relationship between their writing and drawing subtly shifts. Earlier in the literacy learning process, children's meaning resides more in their talk and drawing than in their writing. Take Claude's work for example: At the beginning of the school year, he writes his name to claim ownership of the drawing, and then again to label one of the figures he's drawn. That's it. Yet, by the end of the year, Claude writes to his pen pal that he and his classmates "aRe Stolrice [studying] A But Space." In his pen pal letter, the writing occupies three-quarters of the page, with his drawings in a band along the top, almost as decoration.

◇ As they increasingly control the writing system, young writers develop enough perspective on their writing to begin to revise it. At
first, this perspective manifests itself as merely scratching out a letter
or two that doesn't seem to work. By late fall or early spring, Vincent,
Hicham, Claude, and Mira are all scratching out letters, if not whole
words. Mira does this even in her first work of the year (Figure 5-2).
In a more complex act of revision in late spring, Mira adds a whole
line (six words) to her pen pal letter when she realizes her writing
doesn't express the full message she intends.

HOW TO EXPLAIN THE CHILDREN'S
PROGRESS IN ACQUIRING LITERACY?

Literacy learning requires confidence on the kids' part—confidence
that their writing means what they say it means—and confidence
on the teacher's part that the kids' literacy *will* become increasingly
conventional. In part, the kids' confidence depends on the encouragement they get from others, both peers and teachers. It also
depends on the assistance they get from others, who help them do
what they cannot do on their own.

When the children know they can count on receiving the assistance they need to accomplish the task at hand—*Write a letter to
your pen pal*, or *In your journal, tell about something*—they are willing
to risk testing out their hypotheses about the written language.
They are willing to use invented spelling and not get hung up
on "spelling right." With the assistance they need, and with the
confidence to draw on the available resources, including their own
intuitions, the children sail further into literacy waters.

Also facilitating children's literacy learning are these factors:

◇ The children are given latitude to write what they want, and are
encouraged to do so by their teacher. When children control their
literacy context, their writing is longer and more complex; there is
evidence of hypothesis-testing; their topics are varied; and, frankly,
they themselves are happier, busier, and more productive. In classes
where children's literacy contexts are teacher-controlled, children
write little, fret about spelling, and express only what they think the
teacher wants. I observe some such classes. In a music class, for
instance, when I inquire why children are not writing when given
paper and crayons, I am told that writing will come later after they
know their letters. *First their shapes, then later their letters*, their music
teacher asserts. Believe it or not, this is Mira, Claude, Vincent, and

Hicham's class he's talking about. (Huss, 1995, writes of finding the same distinctions between student-controlled and teacher-controlled literacy contexts, and their subsequent influences on children's literacy development.)

◇ The children are free, even encouraged, to engage in productive chatter with their peers—to talk in *any* language—as they work on a task. (Huss, 1995, finds the role of peer talk, as children work at the writing table, to be *more* important than teacher talk.) Kids consult on drawings, ask each other for the spelling of words they need, ask questions that clarify their thinking, share their work, and even critique each other's work (sometimes harshly). Overall, as they talk, they are working collaboratively. Ultimately, this talk provides valuable mentoring to help them do what they cannot do on their own. (Huss agrees; she also cites Cazden, 1982, and Vygotsky, 1978, in support of the importance of peer talk during writing time.)

TWO CRITICAL FACTORS

Although I see literacy learning going on in all kindergarten, pre-first, and first grade classes at CAS, two factors emerge in my understanding of the critical difference between *some* literacy learning and *abundant* literacy learning, even in parallel circumstances. I mean the difference between, say, one child adding a one-word label to her drawing, while another child writes "I LICEIt Be CAS It FanE"—both responding to a request to tell about a story their teachers have read to them, after the same amount of instructional time, but in different literacy learning environments.

The two factors are these: (1) the teacher's intuitive–intellectual sense, finely honed, of the exact nature of the new challenge each child is ready to handle, day by day, and even moment by moment; and (2) the assistance the children receive—*through talk*—in doing what they cannot do on their own. *If* these factors are integral to a teacher's instructional operation, it ultimately matters little, or at least less, whether she adheres to a whole language philosophy or runs a more traditional classroom, with, say, structured exercises and spelling tests. The sense I have made of my experience with the children surprises me. I am a strong believer in whole language.

To be more fully understood, these factors need theoretical grounding. And the only framework that can help explain them is Vygotskyan theory. Bear with me.

Generally stated, Vygotsky (1978) posits the very beginnings of literacy in a child's grasping the symbolic nature of *gesture* (p.

107)—in, say, a wave of the hand to "mean" *bye-bye*, or the equivalent. Gestures are a child's *first-order symbols* (1983, p. 281) in that they represent something different from what they themselves are.*

To Vygotsky, understanding the mystery of writing acquisition lies chiefly in understanding how a child develops a conception of *second-order symbols*, i.e., symbols representing something, which, in turn, represent something else (p. 281). The sounds we make, which we call *speech*, represent things; and writing, in its most elemental form, represents speech, which represents things.

Imaginative play becomes Vygotsky's bridge between the two symbolic worlds, eventually linking gestures to children's scribbling, as early manifestations of literacy. In creative play, children begin creating and manipulating abstract symbols, in that things "become" what children say they are. A doll becomes a baby; a tin can, a space ship; a stick, a horse.

Picking up where Vygotsky leaves off, Luria (1982) connects a child's scribbling to drawing, in which pictures represent actions, people, places, and even whole narratives. A picture, as a *pictograph*, becomes a child's first written symbol. Through social interaction, a child soon grasps that differentiating the marks changes the "meaning." So, with different marks, one pictograph represents a house; another, a tree or a dog.

In another intellectual leap, a child realizes that she can transform pictures into abstract symbols. In other words, she learns she can "draw" words, which have nothing in common with their referent (an actual house, tree, or dog). She probably first draws her name.

With assistance from others, the child grasps the principles that govern the manipulation of these abstract symbols. In an English literacy context, she begins to realize that the symbols represent sounds. And through a process of approximation and adjustment, she gradually fine-tunes her understanding of exactly how the system works. (Steward, 1995, [pp. 11–16] cogently presents a Vygotskyan perspective on literacy.)

KNOWING WHAT CHALLENGES A CHILD IS READY TO MEET

More to the point, for my purposes, is Vygotsky's influential concept of the *zone of proximal development*. The zone is the distance between

---

*I am grateful to Aaron Nitzkin, a graduate student in one of my classes, whose own research helped me understand Vygotsky's work better.

what a child actually knows and can do alone and the child's *potential* for knowing and doing, with some assistance from an adult or in collaboration with more capable peers (Moll, 1990, p. 86; cited in Steward, 1995, p. 13).

Within the framework of my study, such a "space" is exactly what a focused, insightful teacher holds in awareness: exactly what each child knows, at any given moment, and how to position assistance from herself or the child's peers in order to move the child's learning forward. This is what I meant earlier (in Chapter 4, in writing about Melanie and Eileen) by "knowing what each child is ready for, moment by moment, day by day."

As a note of caution, Steward (1995) warns that Vygotsky's work implies that we think of a zone *not* as a characteristic of a child or of the child's teaching. Rather, we understand it as "the child engaged in collaborative activity within specific social environments" (p. 13).

A zone of proximal development is a moving target then. It is actively, indeed interactively, created by a teacher and students. And it can be accessed only within the dynamic social system in which children learn (Rivers, 1988; cited in Steward, p. 13). When I perceive teachers acting on their intuition and insight to assist a child, I am seeing—in Vygotsky's framework—teachers as "agents capable of driving [children's] development and learning" by providing just the right assistance at just the right moment (Tharp & Gallimore, 1988; cited by Steward, p. 13).

Abundant literacy learning is taking place, then, in classrooms where teachers operate within each child's zone. And when the assistance is right, it ultimately doesn't matter if, in terms of a child's success, literacy is intertwined with the child's first or second language.

PROVIDING THE RIGHT ASSISTANCE

The metaphor of *scaffolding* (Cazden, 1982; Bruner, 1985) is often used to refer to the graduated assistance children get to help them accomplish what they cannot do on their own. I too use the metaphor in thinking and writing about the children and teachers who share their classrooms with me. But I agree with Steward (p. 14) that the metaphor is limited. It can connote a kind of *uniform* assistance—even kinds of something-to-be-taught class "lessons." Neither is what I see in the most successful literacy learning classrooms.

The successful assistance I see differs from child to child. It even differs from activity to activity for the *same* child. In other words, the assistance is not uniform for each child for each activity. I doubt if it is *consciously* tailor-made by a teacher, and it certainly can't be preplanned. But it is tailor-made nevertheless. Assistance might manifest itself as a word of encouragement, *Good job!* Or as a directive, *Write "Dear . . ." on the first line of your pen pal letter.* Or as the answer to a question, *Here's how to spell* gurney; *I'll write it on this paper, and you can copy it.* And so on. Successful assistance often comes from a teacher, or her aide, but it can as easily come from a child's peer.

Assistance provided to children within their respective zones of proximal development—that is, helping *them* accomplish what they cannot do on their own—this is what I see in successful literacy learning classrooms. But this understanding is still too general to capture precisely what is going on in the classes I am participating in.

My mind is awash with questions. Exactly what key mechanism drives literacy learning forward? That is, what causes just the right assistance to shift the zone "upward," so that the subsequent assistance needs to be qualitatively different to enable the child to learn something even more complex? What *about* the nature of the assistance is crucial? What is it exactly that makes the *right* assistance *right*?

After much reflection, I realize, with dawning awareness, that the common denominator in the *most* successful literacy learning classrooms is the *verbal nature* of the assistance. Not only is the assistance individualized, it is verbally manifested. This is the key mechanism. I almost miss it, but it's right before my ears.

It's not just that the most successful teachers help children accomplish difficult literacy tasks, but they tailor-make their assistance *and* their talk to the individual child. (Chapter 5 discusses teaching.) It's as if there are two realities—two domains—in these classrooms: one, the lessons, understood as content, or even know-how; *and* the other, an almost-out-of-awareness arena of reflective, affective, and mediative talk that serves to assist each child in managing the first domain.

Since I figure this out after gaining enough time and space for reflective distance on my experience, I comb through my notes and writings for clues to the level of conscious awareness these teachers have about the nature of talk and its role in their teaching. Their awareness is evident, although each one characterizes it in her own way. Time and again in our discussions, Marge foregrounds the role of "metalanguage" in *her* teaching: helping children develop a language-about-language in order to talk about writing, reading, language, and learning. "Metalanguage" as a language for ideas, information, know-how, and reflection. For Patricia, it's "critical dialoguing," as a medium for helping her kids step back and talk about what they're doing and learning. For Eileen and Melanie, it's "talk about talk," as they mediate children's language and literacy learning processes.

VERBAL MEDIATION

What I think of as "verbally manifested, individualized assistance," Steward (1995) calls *verbal mediation* (p. 77). Heath calls it critically important *talk about talk* and *talk about "nothing"* (1991).

The upshot is that first- *and* second-language children accomplish literacy best in classrooms where they and their teachers talk about their learning, talk about writing and written language, talk about all aspects of language. Children and their teachers step back and look at what they're doing, and then talk about it. They process everything verbally. They talk about what they will do, are doing, and have done. And why. While, by necessity, a lot of teacher talk is directed to the whole class, the most effective assistance is, ultimately, verbally tailored for and to each child.

Children are verbally and individually mentored into learning, into literacy. This individualized, verbal mentoring is, then, the engine that drives learning, the engine that constructs new zones of proximal development. It's as simple—and as complex—as that.

The classroom adult moves in and out of two domains, moment by moment, playing both the role of teacher—presenting, explaining, directing lessons/activities—and the role of mediator—intervening, when and where needed, to bring the child and the "lesson" together. The first domain is traditionally "there" in a classroom; the second, the teacher has to know *to* create and then know *how* to create. The construction of the second is impossible without a teacher's awareness of the possibility of its creation.

If we think about it, verbal mediation, to use Steward's term, takes place in many of the actions and activities that we readily associate with "progressive" writing instruction contexts anyway: peer editing, cross-age tutoring, writing conferences, cooperative writing, "publishing" writing, dialogue journals, and collaborative writing projects. Maybe we've just not realized that the same mechanism is also crucial for very young children whose literacy has not manifested itself so fully.

Verbal mediation does not dictate a teacher's methodology per se. While my heart lies with whole language, children in more traditional classrooms with teachers who focus on what each needs and mediates the assistance through talk are also becoming abundantly literate. An absence of verbal mediation in providing assistance within a child's zone, and thereby creating a new zone, would account for why some classrooms don't work well for literacy learning, even if they are, for all intents and purposes, whole language classrooms. No matter how taught, noncooperative classrooms restrict early literacy learning. Silent classrooms stifle it altogether.

NOTE ON LANGUAGE AND LITERACY LEARNING

I said earlier that I wasn't sure how far the analogy between emergent language and emergent literacy would take me. I see now that it only takes me so far.

Language acquisition for young first- and second-language children is an internal, developmental process. It is triggered, and then driven, *through* language interaction. I don't mean to minimize its complexity, but, given half a chance, young children *will* acquire the language around them.

Literacy learning is not "bound" to happen nearly so easily. For one, it is more complexly symbolic. While oral language is symbolic too—that is, it is representational—written language is symbolic of symbolic oral language—representational of how we might represent something if we were to choose an oral medium.

While written language is representational of oral language, writing remains, only briefly, oral language "written down." At most, written language is *intertwined* with oral language. Once a young child makes the alphabetic connection (for English writing, that is), literacy development begins to take on a life of its own, settling into a coexistence with oral language.

On the relationship between oral and written language, Steward concludes that the "path to literacy is not *through* oral language, but *side by side* with it . . ." (emphasis Steward's, 1995, p. 5). Scinto (1986) speculates that "If it were the case that written language were merely a notational variant of oral language . . . the emergence of written language . . . would proceed far more rapidly . . . having as it were a basis for imitation, and should at any stage . . . reflect the state of the child's oral language development" (p. 68; cited in Nitzkin, 1996). Written language does not "just" reflect the state of a child's oral development, which explains why children still new to English can move ahead with literacy learning, even in English-medium classrooms.

With language learning and literacy learning, the nature of each beast is profoundly different. Very generally put, the process of language learning happens from the inside out. While it must be triggered externally, and comprehensible input must be socially provided, the mechanisms that drive language learning, and the capacity for it, seem to be biological and developmental.

On the other hand, literacy learning, depending so heavily on external social and cultural contexts, happens from the outside in. Writing itself has not been on the human landscape long enough for its learning to be biologically rooted. While language learning seems to depend on, even construct, individuals as social beings, literacy learning seems the converse: It depends on social beings undergoing a process of individualization.

◆ REFERENCES

Bruner, J. V. (1985). *Vygotsky: A historical and conceptual perspective.* In J. V. Wertsch (Ed.), *Culture, communication, and cognition: Vygotskian perspectives* (pp. 21–34). Cambridge, England: Cambridge UP.

Cazden, C. (1982). Adult assistance to language development: Scaffolds, models and direct instruction. In R. Parker & F. David (Eds.), *Developing literacy: Young children's use of language* (pp. 3–18). Newark, DE: International Reading Association.

Clay, M. M. (1966). *Emergent reading behaviour.* Unpublished doctoral dissertation, University of Auckland, New Zealand.

Cummins, J. (1984). *Bilingualism and special education: Issues in assessment and pedagogy.* Clevedon, England: Multilingual Matters.

Ferreiro, E. (1991). Literacy acquisition and the representation of language. In C. Kamii, M. Manning, & G. Manning (Eds.), *Early literacy: A constructivist foundation for whole language* (pp. 31–55). Washington, DC: National Education Association.

Ferreiro, E., & Teberosky, A. (1982). *Literacy before schooling.* Portsmouth, NH: Heinemann.

Freeman, D. E. & Freeman, Y. S. (1994). *Between worlds: Access to second language acquisition.* Portsmouth, NH: Heinemann.

Freeman, Y. S., & D. E. (1992). *Whole language for second language learners.* Portsmouth, NH: Heinemann.

Heath, S. B. (1991). A lot of talk about nothing. In B. M. Power & R. Hubbard (Eds.), *Literacy in process* (pp. 79–87). Portsmouth, NH: Heinemann.

Huss, R. L. (1995). Young children becoming literate in English as a second language. *TESOL Quarterly, 29*(4), 767–774.

Krashen, S. (1982). *Principles and practice in second language acquisition.* New York: Pergamon Press.

Luria, A. R. (1982). *Language and cognition.* New York: Wiley.

Moll, L. C. (Ed.). (1990). *Vygotsky and education: Instructional implications and applications of sociohistorical psychology.* Cambridge, MA: Cambridge UP.

Nitzkin, A. (1996). *The metaphorical roots of writing.* Unpublished research paper, English Department, University of New Orleans.

Rivers, W. J. (1988). *Problems in composition: A Vygotskian perspective.* Unpublished doctoral dissertation, University of Delaware, Newark.

Scinto, L. E. M. (1986). *Written language and psychological development.* New York: Academic Press.

Steward, E. P. (1995). *Beginning writers in the zone of proximal development.* Hillsdale, NJ: Lawrence Erlbaum.

Teale W. H., & Sulzby, E. (Eds.). (1986). *Emergent literacy: Writing and reading.* Norwood, NJ: Ablex.

Tharp, R. G., & Gallimore, R. (1988). *Rousing minds to life.* Cambridge, MA: Cambridge UP.

Vygotsky, L. S. (1978). *Mind in society: The development of higher psychological processes.* Cambridge, MA: MIT Press.

Yule, G. (1996). *The study of language, 2/e.* Cambridge, MA: Cambridge UP.

◆ RELATED REFERENCES: FOR FURTHER READING

Blazer, B. (1986). I want to talk to you about writing: Five year olds speak. In B. Schiefflin & P. Gilmore (Eds.), *The acquisition of literacy: Ethnographic perspectives, vol. XXI: Advances in discourse processes* (pp. 75–109). Norwood, NJ: Ablex.

Dyson, A. H. (1984). Emerging alphabetic literacy in school contexts: Towards defining the gap between school curriculum and child mind. *Written Communication, 1,* 5–55.

Dyson, A. H., (Ed.). (1989a). *Collaboration through writing and reading: Exploring possibilities.* Urbana, IL: National Council of Teachers of English.

Dyson, A. H. (1989b). *Multiple worlds of childhood writers: Friends learning to write.* New York: Teachers College Press.

Dyson, A. H. (1993). *Social worlds of children learning to write in an urban primary school*. New York: Teachers College Press.

Goodman, Y. (1989). Roots of the whole-language movement. *The Elementary School Journal, 90*, 114–127.

Goodman, Y. (Ed.). (1990). *How children construct literacy.* Newark, DE: International Reading Association.

Harste, J. C., Woodward, V. A., & Burke, C. L. (1984). *Language stories and literacy lessons*. Portsmouth, NH: Heinemann.

Heath, S. B. (1982). Ethnography in education: Defining the essentials. In P. Gilmore & A. A. Glatthorn (Eds.), *Children in and out of school: Ethnography and education* (pp. 33–55). Washington, DC: Center for Applied Linguistics.

Heath, S. B. (1986). Critical factors in literacy development. In S. deCastell, A. Luke, & K. Egan (Eds.), *Literacy, society, & schooling: A reader* (pp. 209–229). New York: Cambridge UP.

Hudelson, S. (1986). ESL children writing: What we've learned, what we're learning. In P. Rigg & D. S. Enright (Eds.), *Children and ESL: Integrating perspectives* (pp. 25–54). Washington, DC: TESOL.

Hudelson, S. (1989). *Write on: Children's writing in ESL*. Englewood Cliffs, NJ: Prentice-Hall Regents.

Hymes, D. (1974). *Foundations of sociolinguistics: An ethnographic approach*. Philadelphia: University of Pennsylvania Press.

Sulzby, E. (1985). Kindergartners as writers and readers. In M. Farr (Ed.), *Advances in writing research, volume one: Children's early writing development* (pp. 127–199). Norwood, NJ: Ablex.

Sulzby, E. (1986). Writing and reading: Signs of oral and written language organization in the young child. In W. H. Teale & E. Sulzby (Eds.), *Emergent literacy: Writing and reading* (pp. 50–89). Norwood, NJ: Ablex.

Wertsch, J. V. (1984). The zone of proximal development: Some conceptual issues. In B. Rogoff & J. V. Wertsch (Eds.), *Children's learning in the "zone of proximal development"* (pp. 3–21). San Francisco, CA: Jossey-Bass.

◆ THOUGHT STARTERS
for reflection, journal writing, and/or discussion:

1. Describe an early writing experience. How would you characterize it? How did others respond? Any other memorable writing experiences, good or bad?

2. If the early-language and literacy acquisition models are valid, why must there be a tolerance for "error"? How is this view different from past notions about usage errors?

3. How may the concepts of "zones" and "verbal mediation" conflict with approaches in which students quietly do "book work"?

4. Apply the notions of "zones" and "verbal mediation" to your own experiences teaching and learning (in or out of school).

5. What are the implications for teaching of Blanton's findings on verbal mediation? Implications for teacher training?

◆ PROJECT STARTERS
for writing and research:

1. Become buddies with a child learning to write and read. Keep a journal (over a brief time) of her/his progress. Write up your experience in an ethnographic account, noting differences in and/or similiarities to the work of the kids in Chapter 6.

2. Review three to four journal articles on Vygotskyan theory, especially related to second literacy acquisition. Summarize your findings and relate them to teaching/learning.

3. Review three to four journal articles on the role of *talk* in language and/or literacy instruction. Critique the articles in light of your own experience. Does the role of talk change if L2 students are already literate in L1?

4. Observe the class of a teacher whose students, you think, are "blossoming" into language and/or literacy. Write an account.

Chapter Seven

The Buddy System: Third Graders Write and Read through Cross-Age Tutoring

With Ann Manring*

There is one . . . kind of borrowing [that] is more nebulous, but I catch glimmers. It is the way literature permeates the lives of kids who read and write. They borrow from their readings not just for writing; the ways they walk, talk, and look at the world are subtly altered.

—Nanci Atwell,
In the Middle

LOOKING FOR WAYS TO ALTER THEIR WORLD

I like my buddy a lot and I am very happy with my buddy. I'll never forget my buddy! I hop [hope] I'll never have a different buddy! Anouk, a student in Ann's third grade class at the Casablanca American School, expresses well how most of her classmates feel about their cross-age tutoring program. Forty-minute weekly meetings provide them with an opportunity to learn responsibility and develop friendships with four-year-olds—their *buddies* in Melanie's kindergarten class. Working with their young buddies also provides Ann's third graders with opportunities and real purposes for writing and reading.

During Ann's four years at the Casablanca American School, she

---

*This chapter was cowritten with Ann Manring, the third grade teacher whose experience it is about. Ann was in her fourth year of teaching at the Casablanca American School when she and Linda Blanton collaborated on a cross-age tutoring program between Ann's class and Melanie Wong Jones's kindergartners. Ann is now teaching in the Greater Albany (Oregon) public schools.

has searched for teaching strategies to meet what she sees as the children's special needs. Some needs stem from children's limited responsibilities outside of school: Since many come from well-to-do homes, with a staff to wait on the family, the children's sole "job" at home may be their homework, and that without parental supervision. The buddy system seems a good way for Ann to help her kids build a greater sense of responsibility to others, as well as put them in the spotlight of others' attention.

The rigorous curriculum at the Casablanca American School poses another challenge for Ann's students. Located in the largest city in Morocco, CAS is a nursery to twelfth grade school with a student body of about four hundred, over half of them Moroccan. The rest come from countries around the globe—Holland, Belgium, France, Korea, Germany, England, the Philippines, Vietnam, the United States—and few are first language speakers of English.

When CAS students reach eleventh grade, they can opt for an extremely demanding plan of study leading to an International Baccalaureate (IB), a program similar to Advanced Placement study in the United States. CAS is the first school in North Africa to offer an IB curriculum, which gives students and their families greater options for post-secondary study. With an IB in hand, students can seek admission to universities in many parts of the world. With only an American-style diploma, they would be limited to the United States. Most families opt for the IB plan of study.

As well as needing to manage a difficult curriculum in English, most CAS students, beginning in the third grade, spend 80 minutes a day studying French and Arabic, the home languages of the Moroccan students. With little to no English spoken at home, most CAS students' engagement with English is limited to school.

Ann's third grade class is a microcosm of this great linguistic and cultural mix. In a class of 18, there are eleven Moroccans, two French, one Belgian, one Filipino, one Kuwaiti, and two Americans, one of whom is bilingual (English/French). Although most have been at CAS since nursery school, two of the students arrived last year and one is in his first year of English. Ann's planning must always take into account her students' varying levels of fluency in English.

FINDING THE COURAGE TO BEGIN

I hate my buddy! Hicham proclaims to Ann soon after the new buddy program begins. This is a problem she is not prepared to handle. *I want a new buddy!* After all of Ann's careful planning, she assumed all students would instantly love their new friends. She can't believe Hicham wants to trade his in like a used car. Sometimes quick—often too quick— to doubt her own intuitions about teaching, Ann's belief in the value of cross-age tutoring is suddenly shaken. What should she do? Keep Hicham out of the activity? Isn't one of the major reasons for doing buddies to build self-esteem and promote responsibility? How much responsibility can Hicham learn if he makes no emotional investment in his buddy?

After discussing Hicham's problem and her own self-doubts with Melanie, *her* teacher-buddy in the partner kindergarten class, Ann decides Hicham *should* participate in the tutoring program for the very reason he doesn't want to. She asks him to write three things he can do to get along better with his buddy and three actions Ann and Melanie can take, as teachers, to help him.

In response, Hicham writes that he can pay more attention to his buddy, listen to his buddy better, and find out what his buddy's interests are. His advice for Ann and Melanie is to change his buddy. But if that isn't possible, they should help him create fun activities for his buddy and also let him work with his third grade classmates to plan activities together for their buddies. Ann thinks Hicham's advice is sound and she proceeds to implement it, hoping all the while that Hicham adjusts and his buddy doesn't suffer.

READING ABOUT CROSS-AGE TUTORING

Although Ann firmly believes that Hicham needs to be part of the buddy program, she feels more confident with others' experience to back her up. In the literature, she discovers that teachers working with reluctant readers and/or managing large classes without assistance are turning to cross-age tutoring as one solution to providing activities that encourage literacy (Cook & Urzua, 1993; Labbo & Teale, 1990; Rekrut, 1994). Though Ann's class is relatively small, 18 students, and their attitudes toward learning are generally positive, she needs new ways to encourage language and literacy to offset her children's lack of access to English at home and their likely lack of literacy interaction with others outside of school.

One theme recurs throughout Ann's reading: Children should be involved in authentic and meaningful literacy activities. In other words, writing and reading should be part of completing tasks children are interested in accomplishing (Graves, 1983; Atwell, 1987; Calkins, 1994; Samway *et al.*, 1995).

Leland and Fitzpatrick (1993), emphasizing the importance of providing literate opportunities that are enjoyable, find that their sixth graders, low readers generally uninterested in reading, develop positive reading attitudes by the end of their yearlong collaborative tutoring program. The older students read aloud to their young buddies and discuss book and author choices among themselves. By year's end, they are checking out more books from the library and reading eagerly.

Another journal article, focusing on student athletes and their at-risk tutees, stresses the self-confidence the younger children gain while working with the athletes (Juel, 1991). The athletes in turn become more engaged in reading and journal writing.

Heath and Mangiola's work (1991) is especially helpful to Ann. Outlining a plan for cross-age tutoring with a variety of reading and writing activities, they advise training time for students and an occasional review of reading and writing techniques. They recommend meeting regularly with tutors to discuss their tutees' progress. And they include a question-and-answer section that Ann finds useful as she begins a cross-grade tutoring program.

Ann's reading convinces her that cross-age tutoring is worthwhile for several reasons. And, to get herself started and focused on her goals, she iterates the reasons:

◇ Her students need self-esteem building.

◇ They require more opportunities for writing and reading.

◇ Few of her students read at home and tutoring is a way of encouraging reading.

◇ As nonnative speakers of English, they need to build oral English-language skills, especially in giving directions, explaining word meanings, and discussing ideas.

◇ And, finally, her students can only benefit from weekly responsibilities.

Though Ann doesn't fully appreciate it when beginning the buddy program, her students increasingly become invested in planning their own learning, gain experience in creating learning contexts for themselves and their buddies, and learn to evaluate their own teaching/learning as well. And, as the year progresses, Ann's conception of language arts evolves into writing and reading as *social interaction*, with the classroom as a setting for purposeful literate activities.

Coming to the realization that cross-age tutoring is beneficial, Ann believes, is the first step to a successful program. The second step is developing a close and compatible working relationship with the teacher–partner of the tutees. Ann is fortunate to have developed such a relationship with Melanie, one of the kindergarten teachers. They share similar views on teaching, which makes organizing and planning smooth and enjoyable. To discuss and plan the upcoming week, Ann and Melanie generally meet once or twice a week, for 15 to 20 minutes.

PAIRING BUDDIES

After deciding to begin a buddy program, Ann and Melanie first meet to develop a general plan and pair up their kids. They decide to have buddies from the two classes meet every week on the same day at the same time for about 35 minutes, believing that routine is important to the success of the program. After a month or two into it, when they need to skip a week, students ask, *Why aren't we having buddies today?* or *When will we make it up?* Ann and Melanie know then that students are hooked.

To pair buddies, Ann and Melanie proceed on the basis of personality and language skills. Since most of the third grade Moroccans speak English, French, and Arabic, they are matched up with students who speak little or no English, so those new to English won't be left out. Ann's native English speaker, who knows no French, is paired with Melanie's kindergarten child whose English skills are strong, so these two can communicate well.

Ann and Melanie also pair strong-willed children, and this seems a good decision, since timid children sometimes have trouble managing younger ones. Finally, boys are paired with boys and girls with girls, which ultimately makes no difference in how well the children work together, Melanie and Ann later decide.

As families move to and from Casablanca, the buddy partners change. One kindergarten student begins with two third grade buddies. Two students in third grade leave and two arrive in kindergarten. So some third graders end up with two buddies. If a student is absent, his or her buddy joins another buddy dyad or triad. These changes, however, don't seem to affect students' attitudes towards buddies. They still look forward to buddy time, whether they're with their regular partner or not.

Before the first meeting with buddies, Ann and her students discuss what they think is expected of them as tutors. Ann mentions that they are responsible for their buddy's experience—that they, in effect, are teachers. Whatever they do, their young buddy will do. If they run around the room, their buddy will too. Monkey see, monkey do. Ann emphasizes that the kindergarten kids are only four years old and physically can't do all a third grader can do. In fact, they might hurt themselves if they try. Ann thinks her third graders have responded well to these concerns and are conscientious about setting good examples.

KEEPING A BUDDY JOURNAL

When asked later in the year, *Have you done writing you think is special? If so, what makes it special?* Mariam, a third grader, responds, *My unique writing is my buddy book because I write more paragraphs.* She also writes, *I like my buddy book because we do activities and we write what we like about them.*

From the beginning of the tutoring program, third graders keep a journal they call their *buddy book* (Bromley, 1995). As a regular part of the schedule and always after their buddy time, Ann's kids discuss the day's activities and then write about them. Ann responds to their journal entries each week, and she finds the entries help her gauge how engaged the third graders are—and how well they're getting along with their partners.

At first, Ann isn't sure how to go about responding to students' journals. In looking for guidance, she reads Atwell (1987), who provides her with sample responses. Atwell convinces Ann that responses motivate kids to read, provide a model for writing, and help them understand what they're thinking and feeling. They can also encourage kids to solve problems and suggest new ways of doing so (Wollman–Bonilla, 1991).

Ann thinks student journals and the teacher's involvement with them are an important part of a tutoring program. Through their journals, Ann's third graders evaluate the activities they've planned and continually analyze their relationship with their buddy. Buddy journals also provide them with a forum for expressing their own concerns (Peyton & Reed, 1990).

In his journal, Mehdi talks about his buddy, Dalila:

Feb. 16, 1995
Today went well because Dalila drew well and understood the story. Next time,
instead of taking one paper to draw, I'll make a whole book.

Ann responds:

Mehdi, I like the idea of a book. Maybe she could draw pictures and you could
write something about each picture in the book. Then she would have her own
book that you two had made together. Mrs. M.

In her journal, Coral responds to Ann's questions *How did buddy*
time go today? What went especially well? and *What will you do next*
time?:

March 17, 1995
Yes, my buddy loved it [.] her favorite part was when the enemy fell in the
dungeon. When she said dungoen I didn't know what that word ment so Camille
tought me something [.] I know that she likes the book because she paid attention
because she wanted to do the activity.

I told [asked] her wich picture she liked [.] she said she liked when the man fell
in the dungeon.

I will try to paint more because she likes painting.

Ann thinks her third graders are good about honestly reflecting
on what they've done. Even though they aren't always keen on
writing in their journals, Ann doesn't hear many complaints. As
in Coral's journal entry above, Ann's third graders often respond
to prompts such as these:

◇   *What went well?*
◇   *What would you do differently?*
◇   *Did you enjoy the activity? Why or Why not?*
◇   *Did anything exciting happen today?*
◇   *What will you do next time?*

But, as the school year progesses, Ann's prompts evolve, and by
the end, she is asking more analytic questions such as:

◇   *What kinds of questions did you ask your buddy while you were reading?*
◇   *If the director walked in, how might he describe your activity?*
◇   *How did your buddy respond to today's activities?*

◇   *Would you recommend the book you read and the activity you did to other tutors? Why or Why not?*

INITIAL BUDDY-TIME ACTIVITIES

The first few times buddies meet, activities are simple and aimed at getting to know each other. At the first meeting, everyone sits together and Melanie reemphasizes what Ann has told the third graders about being teachers to their kindergarten buddies. Buddies are then introduced to each other and head outside to play together for about 15 minutes. This gives them a little time to get acquainted in the more casual environment of the playground. The next week, third graders read to their buddies books they have selected from the library and brought to the kindergarten room.

At the beginning of the year the activities are all planned by Melanie and Ann. Melanie plans one week and Ann, the next. They plan activities integrated with the lessons in their separate classwork. When the third graders are studying about architecture, for example, buddy activities include creating symmetrical designs out of pattern blocks and making mosaics out of paper. Though these seem like excellent activities, they *belong* to the teachers, and the third graders' interest wanes, since they have invested no time or energy in the planning.

Although Ann feels early on that the cross-grade tutoring program is a social and affective success, she is slow to grasp how effective a reading and writing tool it can be, despite the emphasis on literacy in her readings on collaborative learning. She keeps tripping on the perception that the third graders' higher level of language and literacy directs all the benefits to the kindergartners. Not until she sees Mohamed's difficulty in reading to his kindergarten buddy does she realize more fully the potential for the older kids.

A SPIN-OFF TUTORING PROGRAM FOR SHAKY READERS

Early in the school year, Mohamed and his buddy, Soufiane, pick out *Five Little Monkeys Sitting on a Bed* for Mohamed to read aloud during the time left after a drawing activity. Even though Mohamed already participates in the pull-out remedial reading program, Ann is surprised by the degree of his difficulty in reading to Soufiane.

Like a bolt of lightning, Ann is struck by the obvious: that her third graders need the reading opportunities afforded by the tutoring program as much as, if not more than, the kindergarten kids.

After school that day, Ann talks to Melanie about Mohamed's difficulty. Suddenly sure Mohamed is not the only one with such reading difficulties, Ann still can't believe she didn't notice.

Melanie suggests additional buddy time for the remedial readers. And, since much of Ann's study of cross-age tutoring involves older students with reading problems paired with younger children learning to read, Ann decides Melanie is right. She now starts focusing on cross-age tutoring from the perspective of benefits to the older kids. It gives them a real reason to read aloud to an eager audience, she reasons. Plus, it should be an enormous ego boost to kids like Mohamed.

Ann and Melanie then meet with Sue, a reading teacher, and suggest that the third graders in Sue's pull-out remedial reading class read regularly to kindergarten kids, other than their regular buddies. This would give readers like Mohamed a double dose of cross-age tutoring.

Interested in the possiblilities and with the blessings of Ann and the other third grade teacher, Sue arranges with Melanie to have the third grade remedial readers—five from Ann's class and three from the other third grade class—read to Melanie's *morning* kindergarten kids, a different group from the afternoon buddies that Ann's kids are already working with. Sue sets the plan in motion by working out a schedule: third graders choose their books on Mondays and practice them for homework, before reading to their new buddies on Tuesday mornings.

The remedial readers—Sue calls them *Turbo readers*—read to their buddies in Melanie's room and then return to Sue's classroom, without their buddies, to analyze the success of the week's buddy time. In their journals, they focus on follow-up questions third graders might ask the kindergartners about the reading. Sue encourages them to ask questions that require complex answers and that prompt the kindergarten kids to recall an event from the story or relate it to personal experience. They come up with some great questions:

◇ *Have you ever . . .* [an event in the story]?
◇ *What is your favorite part of the story? Why?*
◇ *Who is your favorite character? Why?*
◇ [Holding up a picture from the story] *What is happening here?*

In his journal, Hamza talks about his Tuesday morning reading time with his buddy:

3/28/95

My buddy liked the book because he tould me. "I like it." I asked him what is this or what is that. Like the dog[.] I tould him what is it. I think I woud not read agin Henry and Mudge.

Later, Hamza writes about reading *The Principal's New Clothes* to his buddy Ghali and then writing a letter to Mr. Randolph, the CAS director, with Ghali's assistance:

May 6, 1995

My buddy learned the polines [?]. I have learned to be pacions [patient] with little kids. Yesterday was the best one because we made a carde for Mr. Randoulph it was realy fun.

Ann responds:

May 6, 1995

Dear Hamza,
  You two were so cute giving that card to Mr. Randolph. I think Ghali greatly enjoyed that.
  You have worked so well with Ghali this year. You're extremely patient with him and the activities you plan are interesting. Keep up the good work!
  Mrs. M.

Ann, Melanie, and Sue hope that by having the shaky readers analyze their questioning techniques, they will begin to ask *themselves* the same kinds of questions when doing their own reading. Sue especially feels that collaborative reading is beneficial to the Turbo readers. They feel more adequate as readers as they bask in the glory of their buddy's attention, Sue thinks. Plus, the new arrangement gives the older kids a *grown-up* reason to read aloud and a goal for which they need to practice reading at home the night before their performance.

ACTIVITIES TO KEEP YOUNGER CHILDREN'S ATTENTION

Whether during the Tuesday morning reading time, for the Turbo readers, or the regular afternoon buddy time, the third graders sometimes find it difficult to keep the kindergartners' attention.

Under Ann's direction, they continually brainstorm ways to maintain the little kids' interest, and, from time to time, Ann models reading aloud.

In addition to asking engaging questions, the third graders practice changing their voices for different story characters and directing their buddy's attention to the story pictures. Ann encourages them to know their reading books well enough so they can *tell* the reading, that is, read in a conversational tone. Together, they decide it's important not to choose long stories, lest their young charges drift off.

To keep buddy sessions lively, the third graders brainstorm the following activities, some of which they manage to complete by the year's end:

◇   *Write our own book and read it to the kindergarten kids.*

◇   *Write book reviews about the books we plan to read to whet our buddy's appetite.*

◇   *Write a pamphlet encouraging parents to read to their children at home, so the kinder kids gain additional experience in being read aloud to.*

◇   *Help our buddy draw or paint pictures to accompany a story.*

◇   *Work with our buddy to create puppets (paper figures glued to sticks) of the story characters and then have the buddy retell the story with the puppets.*

◇   *Make story characters out of clay and retell the story with clay figures.*

◇   *Two buddies retell the story to another pair of buddies.*

◇   *Listen to our buddy tell a story, write the story down, and then read the story to our buddy.*

◇   *Cut letters from a magazine to make a collage of the story title. Paste them on colored paper and then, with our buddy, add drawings to illustrate the story.*

PERIODIC CHECK ON PROGRESS OF THE PROGRAM

Several months into the year, Ann begins to notice that her third graders seem to be getting more excited about reading. Those in Sue's Turbo Reading program conscientiously take their books home to practice for the morning reading time with their buddies. One student volunteers to Ann that he thinks having a buddy makes him a better reader. Ann is pleased.

One day, while Ann and her third graders are in the library, Saad, who doesn't read much on his own and usually checks out easy cartoon books when asked to choose, shows Ann a nonfiction book about lions he's chosen from the shelf. Since Melanie's kinder kids are studying the letter *L* and the third graders are planning lion activities, Saad said, *Mrs. Manring, look what book I found. I'm going to read it to my buddy. It's about lions.* To Ann, this is proof the buddy program is motivating her students to read.

Although pleased overall, Ann constantly frets about the buddy program. Concerned that it's too teacher-centered, with her and Melanie doing much of the planning, she wants students to feel more invested, more involved. She wants some of the less interested students to show more interest. And she wants the whole class to think about their buddies more often than during their once-a-week planning period.

Ultimately what she wants from her third graders is commit-ment—real emotional attachment to their buddy work, the kind that can only come from inside them. Everything Ann reads about the success of cross-age tutoring makes her start thinking that she'll only get it if she puts the third graders in charge, but she finds it hard to let go.

LETTING GO: THIRD GRADERS TAKE OVER
THE PLANNING OF BUDDY TIME

Feeling that the third graders participating in cross-age reading through the Turbo program are more engaged in reading than before—and they have a hand in planning their buddy time—Ann sets out to give all her third graders greater latitude in choosing the books they read to their buddy. Plus she charges them with figuring out ways to incorporate more writing.

To strengthen their reading techniques, Ann and her third grad-ers role-play reading aloud. She plays the teacher; a third grader plays a kinder buddy. He pretends not to understand, to not pay attention, while Ann models methods to keep him on task. Then they change roles.

Afterwards, the third graders discuss techniques they think work best and list them in their buddy books. Brainstorming the types of books they think will best keep the interest of four-year-olds, they create a list of activities to follow reading. They end their planning session by choosing a book, practicing the reading of it, and planning a related activity.

It was the first time I felt like a real teacher, Anouk writes in her journal, after taking over the planning of their buddy time. She expresses the general attitude the third graders feel about taking buddies over. After they carry out their plans with their buddies, Melanie claims it's the best buddy time the kids have had all year.

One of the best planning discussions, a *quasi* debate, occurs when the third graders plan jumping activities for the kindergartners the following week. Melanie comes to Ann's classroom to brainstorm with them and then leaves, leaving them to decide for themselves which games to choose and plan. Their limits, set by Melanie and Ann, are safety, time, and materials. In groups, the third graders plan games and then present their ideas to their classmates.

Yassine, who normally asks unrelated and sometimes silly questions, suddenly begins to ask serious, thoughtful questions, often pointing out the gaps in a group's plan. Mohamed, acting as self-appointed safety officer, quickly notes if an activity is too dangerous for four-year-olds. Feeling stongly committed to their buddies, the whole third grade class joins the discussion, getting their ideas on record, reasoning through them, and changing their minds if someone persuades them otherwise. Their English flows. Vocabulary expands as they search in the class thesaurus for synonyms of words like *jump*. The phrase *communicating for a purpose and to an audience* becomes real to Ann after learning how well the third graders are doing in refining their ideas for buddy time.

FAVORITE BOOKS TO READ TO BUDDIES

When Ann asks her students which books they think are turning out to be the most successful with their buddies, everyone nominates *Clifford*. Ann thinks they like *Clifford* so much because the author, Norman Bridwell, visited the school last year. Students also mention *Yertle the Turtle*. This is one of the books modeled and discussed in class, and this may have influenced the third graders to choose it. *Curious George*, *The Three Billy Goats Gruff*, *The Principal's New Clothes*, and *The Day Jimmy's Boa Ate the Wash* are other favorites. (See Appendix A.)

Ghita, a third grader, has a hard time choosing books for her Tuesday morning reading partner, Sara. Ghita tells Sue, *Sara always wants to read <u>Mrs. Wishy Washy,</u> no matter what book I bring*. Coral says, *I read turtle books to Camille because she likes turtles*. Overall, the third graders try to choose books on topics they know their buddy is interested in.

A buddy's interest and the availability of books determine which books third graders choose. Sometimes they pick a book from the library during their weekly class time there, but generally they choose from among the books available in the classroom.

Though Ann thinks the third graders should focus exclusively on writing and reading, they often think differently. One week they decide to plan a treasure hunt with clues for the kinder kids. Since Ann has turned it over to them, what else can she do but go along? Relinquishing control to her students is difficult when she feels *her* plan for a weekly reading and writing activity is more beneficial to them. They are, however, very excited about *their* idea and work hard on planning for it. The clues that they eventually settle on are clear and not too difficult. On the day of the hunt, they lead their buddies around, read the clue to them, help them figure out the next location, and then walk with them to the next clue. Their activity is a great success. The third graders are excited about it, and despite Ann's reservations, they *are* planning, reading, and writing.

BRINGING MATH INTO CROSS-AGE TUTORING

If cross-age tutoring is an effective tool for reading and writing, it can also be a powerful tool for teaching math, Ann reasons. The National Council of Teachers of Mathematics (1989) stresses that math should be conceptual. And it should also actively involve students. Teachers need to create an environment that encourages children to explore, develop, test, discuss, and apply ideas. With this in mind, Ann decides to branch out and develop some activities that engage her third graders in working with mathematical concepts and involving their buddies.

In groups of six, Ann's students labor on math projects. One project is to read Tomie de Paola's *Pancakes for Breakfast* and plan a pancake party for Melanie's kinder class. Another is a popcorn party for 100 people, which requires them to plan, calculate, and measure. Motivated by parties with their buddies and invited guests, Ann's class performs a variety of math functions to accomplish their projects. At the pancake party, the chefs are praised by their kinder buddies. Once again, the tutoring program provides an opportunity for a project that is fun and educational.

POLLIWOGS AND OTHER SUCCESSFUL ACTIVITIES

Midpoint in the year, buddy time hits a slump. The third graders have fallen into a routine of choosing books to read to their buddy and then working together on some type of follow-up activity such as painting, clay, and drawing. While the plan has worked well, it is now *old hat* and the buddies are getting bored. Ann is also concerned that the third graders aren't writing enough. So, hoping to reinvigorate their reading and encourage them to write more, Ann models making a book.

Ann reads *The Caterpillar and the Polliwog* to the third graders, discussing questioning techniques before and after reading. The third graders critique Ann's techniques and seem interested in polliwogs, Ann is pleased to note. One student even volunteers to bring some in, which he does a few days later. Ann demonstrates one way to write a book with a young child by asking the child to retell the story as she writes it down. Once written down, the story can be illustrated by the two buddies working together.

To Ann's surprise, some of the third graders seem eager to try the idea. The following Thursday in the kinder classroom, these third graders read their books and write about caterpillars and polliwogs with their buddies. Both Ann and Melanie are impressed by the kinder buddies' rapt attention. Unable to finish before the end of the period, the third graders ask to return on another day to complete the project.

The polliwog story continues. Back in Ann's classroom, her students feed the amphibians, brought in by their classmate, and watch them grow. For the schoolwide science festival, her third graders decide to sing a song about tadpoles turning into frogs. And with their buddies, they cut out and glue together a hopping, paper frog and a frog on a bromeliad plant.

Lions interest the kinder kids. Melanie polls her class, charting what they know and would like to know, and sends the information over to Ann's third graders. After reading the kindergartners' questions, the third graders plan projects to answer them. They spend at least an hour planning plays, talk shows, picture matching, and role-playing—all to do with lions. Some work individually, while others work together, to set up mini-learning centers, rotating the kinder kids from station to station. (See Appendix B for a collaboratively written play, starring lions and written by Hamza, Karima, and Yassine, three third graders. The authors were obviously influenced by *The Lion King*.)

Because of their involvement, Ann's students become more interested in their weekly planning meetings. They decide, though, that planning *every* week is too much work. Sometimes the planning wears them down. And Ann sees that they seem to pour more energy into buddy events when they plan less often.

During one biweekly planning period, they review books full of learning activities and then give themselves the homework assignment of making lists of some of the most interesting possibilities. The next day, they spend about an hour in class selecting activities and planning how to do them.

Ann is continually amazed at the third graders' creativity, interest, and dedication to providing their buddy with the best activities possible. With little prompting from her, their plans always include starting buddy time with a book.

While getting ready for last Thursday's planning session, Mohamed, Adrien, and Hamza began talking about a treasure hunt for their buddies, even brainstorming which little treats they could bring in for their buddies on the day of the hunt. Liz and Coral perused resource books in the classroom, searching for a springtime activity. Perle, who began the year with reading difficulties, started making plans to read *The Big Red Barn*. The next day she brought to the planning session three bingo boards covered with pictures of the animals in the story.

Not only do the third graders write and read to prepare for buddy time, they participate in other buddy-related reading and writing events. They write stories about buddy time for the school newspaper that comes out once a month. When the husband of a kindergarten aide visited Ann's class to talk about his job as a flight attendant, they took notes so they could remember everything to tell their buddies. After Melanie came to Ann's class to talk about food, they began writing in their journals about food they want to prepare as part of a buddy activity. Now, Ann's third graders are beginning to think about almost everything in terms of their buddies.

ASSESSING THE BENEFITS OF THE BUDDY PROGRAM

Ann and Melanie attribute some of the success of buddies to the similarity in their own teaching styles. They accept each other as equals and their students, both third graders and kindergartners, recognize this. Neither teacher dominates the other, and each accepts the other's student discipline, ideas, and suggestions. Melanie isn't afraid to give Ann's students *time-outs,* and Ann disciplines Melanie's students when necessary.

Both teachers believe that designing and modeling activities at the beginning and then leaving the third graders to do their own planning plays a big role in the success of the program. Through modeling, students are able to observe the kinds of activities kinder students like and can do.

Melanie considers the curriculum-related activities integral to the success of the program. Melanie lets Ann's students know the focus of her week's plans for the kinder kids, and they take the focus into account as they plan buddy activities.

As the weeks go by, relationships with buddies grow. Melanie's kindergartners think buddy time is the most exciting part of their week. Right before buddy time on Thursdays, the kindergartners can be heard chanting *Our buddies are coming, our buddies are coming.* Melanie says the kinder kids talk a lot about their buddies and get excited at the mention of buddy time.

When asked to name the benefits of the buddy program to her third graders, Ann comes up with a long list. At the top of it is the claim that her students now work together well and are more responsible individuals. In the beginning, they needed help solving their buddies' behavior problems, and they had to be encouraged to stick with their buddy and set a good example. Now even if, on occasion, one of their plans doesn't work well at first, they make it work by adjusting it in some way. The third graders have developed real friendships with the kinder students. Most of all they're excited about buddy time.

When asked *What have you learned from buddies?* three or four third graders admit they have learned to be patient with younger children and are now able to work better with their brother or sister at home. All students say they enjoy working with buddies. Even Hicham, who—at the beginning of the year—said he hated his buddy, admits that his attitude has changed. Now he even knows how to be patient with his little sister, he claims. Liz remarks that she didn't think it was possible to make friends with someone so young, but she has.

Most of Ann's third graders feel they know how to plan better now. Every two weeks they now predict what will work, plan it, and implement it. After every buddy time, they reflect on the experience, measuring the success of an activity and whether it is worth repeating. Now they exchange ideas and advise each other on what works. Though they may not realize they can do all this, they do understand they're better able to execute a plan effectively.

In part because of buddy time, Ann is sure her third graders are becoming better writers. She is seeing writing that is better organized and more focused—and more of it. Early in the year, one group of third graders attempted a play about the gingerbread man. Despite extra time, they couldn't make much headway. In the end, Ann stepped in as scribe to write as they dictated to her. But, recently, two of the same students (with a third classmate) wrote a play, including characters from *The Lion King*, for their buddies' lion activity. The play was done in half the time. (See Appendix B for the later play.)

At the beginning of the year, for the school newspaper, Perle and Ghita wrote a short article on buddies, which says very little and reads like a list of often unrelated sentences. In February, Mariam wrote an article that better describes the buddy program and includes paragraphs and quotations; interestingly, she uses the strategy of listing everyone's buddy in order to extend her writing. Near the end of the year, Anouk, only in her second year of English-medium schooling, volunteered to write an article on their buddy work. She gives a more complete and complex picture of what happens in cross-age tutoring. And, to extend *her* piece, she employs quotations, a more effective rhetorical stategy than simply listing everyone's name.

All four girls started out the year at about the same level of writing proficiency; and the other three could probably have done as well as Anouk by year's end. Ann sees these examples as indicators of progress: from disorganized and uninteresting to longer, more coherent, and more complex pieces of writing. (The articles are included in Appendix C. Although the comparison is among different writers, Ann thinks it a valid one.)

MAKING IT BETTER NEXT TIME

Although Ann thinks the cross-grade program has been a great achievement, she already sees ways to make it better. There was less reading and writing than she would have liked, but she does have to admit that her third graders wrote and read at unexpected times, especially when planning and implementing their activities.

Although the buddies were basically well paired, two exceptions stand out. Both involve shy third graders paired with talkative kindergartners. The two third graders were unable to gain the upper hand and never really gained the satisfaction of guiding and directing their young tutees. Next time, Ann vows to impress upon herself even more the role that personality plays in the success of a tutoring program.

If she were redoing the year, Ann thinks she would limit the program to reading and writing activities—and let students take it from there. Her students would have been more successful from the beginning, she thinks, if she had provided more modeling in class, since they were always quick to follow her example.

In addition to reading, writing, and modeling more, Ann would set aside more time for third graders to plan and do follow-up activities. They were always pressed for time, and they would have enjoyed more time to discuss the books they were reading to the kinder kids. They also never managed to find time to write book reviews for other classes, which they were interested in doing. Ann also thinks a guide written by the third graders for kindergarten parents, a how-to-read-to-your-child type guide, would have been wonderful, but they never found time to write it. The program, too, once it got going, took much more time than Ann expected. Lack of time and feeling rushed were always problems, she feels.

Next time, Ann wants to investigate what would happen if the third graders were participating in a cross-grade tutoring program with older students at the same time as tutoring the younger kids. Finally, she wonders how collaborative learning could become an aspect of the entire school's curriculum.

Ann's original purpose in developing a buddy program was to promote her students' writing development. They *are* better writers now, she has no doubt, but they have gained so much more. Besides writing and reading, the buddy program has provided her third graders with occasions for cooperating, planning, problem solving, evaluating, building self-esteem, developing patience, and shouldering responsibility.

The buddy program has created real reasons for Ann's third graders to write and read. And they have gained experience in collaborating with their peers to think things through, talk them over, and work them out. The results show—and Ann thinks it's not too much to hope that the effects of the buddy program will be lifelong. Like Atwell (1987), Ann is catching glimmers that the ways her students walk, talk, and look at the world have been subtly altered.

♦ APPENDIX A: THIRD GRADERS' FAVORITE BOOKS TO READ TO BUDDIES

Appleby, E. (1984). *Three Billy Goats Gruff, A Norwegian Folktale.* New York: Scholastic.

Brickloe, J. (1985). *Fireflies.* New York: Scholastic.

Bridwell, N. (1985). *Clifford, the Big, Red Dog.* New York: Scholastic.

Brown, M. W. (1956). *The Big Red Barn.* New York: Scholastic.

Calmenson, S. (1989). *The Principal's New Clothes.* New York: Scholastic.

Christlelow, E. (1991). *Five Little Monkeys Sitting on the Bed.* Boston: Houghton Mifflin.

De Paola, T. (1978). *Pancakes for Breakfast.* Orlando, FL: Harcourt Brace Jovanovich.

Geisel, T. (1950). *Yertle the Turtle.* New York: Random House.

Kent, J. (1982). *The Caterpillar and the Polliwog.* New York: Simon and Schuster.

Noble, T. H. (1980). *The Day Jimmy's Boa Ate the Wash.* New York: Dial.

Rey, H. A. (1941). *Curious George.* Boston: Houghton Mifflin.

♦ APPENDIX B: A PLAY WRITTEN BY THREE THIRD GRADERS FOR THEIR BUDDIES

Narrator: *There once were two lions called Mufasa and Simba. Mufasa was Simba's father. Once Simba was attacked by Shenzi, Benzai and Ed.*

Simba: *Help! Help!*

Mufasa: *I'm coming Simba!*

Shenzi, Benzai and Ed: *I'm scared let's go!*

Narrator: *When Shenzi, Benzai and Ed ran away Simba said "Dad can you play hide and seek with me?"*

Mufasa: *Yes, Simba.*

Narrator: *When Mufasa was playing with Simba[,] Shenzi, Benzai and Ed came and said "1-2-3 go! rrrrrrr.*

Benzai: *That was it!*

Shenzi: *Ha! Ha! Ha!*

Ed: *H,H,H.*

By Hamza, Karima, and Yassine

◆ APPENDIX C: CONTRAST OF THREE PIECES OF WRITING BY THIRD GRADERS

Article for School Newspaper, Written 10/94:

Buddies

3B (Ann's third grade class) *goes to Kinder B all Thursdays. 3B calls kindergartens buddies are litte kids. If someone is bad they are bad. Little kids like buddies do the same thing as you. Some of the kids speak english some of them speak french some of them speak arabic. My buddy speaks french. Some times when I say to my buddy can you draw me a head or some thing like that she tells me I don't no. My buddy is named Tania. With our buddies we did the gingerbred boy story. When we did the gingerbred boy play to.*

By Perle and Ghita

Article for School Newspaper, Written 2/95:

Buddies

Buddies is a kind of project. The project is that a grade of older students in a school comes to another class of younger students class. Who comes to the another class does projects with them like Reading, math and writing. They come every week.

My buddy is Zineb. Liz's buddy is Sara S. Anouk's buddy is Sara A. Perle's buddy is Tania, Karima's buddy is Simonetta, Coral's buddy is Camille, Ghita's buddy is Houda, Mehdi's buddy is Dalila, Hicham's buddy is Mohamed, Hacham's buddy is Ahmed, Mohamed's buddy is Soufiane, Saad A's buddy is Tomo, Saad K's buddy is Othman, Mark's buddy is Hinde, Adrien's buddy is Celine, Hamza's buddy is Ghali, Mustapha's buddy is Yassine and Yassine's buddy is Zakaria.

Some of the activities we've done since January 1995 are a popcorn party, a pancake party, the letter C, read a book, do activity, treasure hunt, pin the tale on the donkey, the jumping activity. Saad A says, "painted read stories draw, some think about." Mohamed says "We've done clay."

By Mariam

Article for School Newspaper, Written 5/95:

The Smartest Kindergarten Buddies

Each Thursday 3B has buddies. We do all kinds of activities in buddies. Sometimes Mrs. Manring decides what we do for buddies and sometimes it's Mrs. Melanie. Sometimes we read books and sometimes we draw pictures and we make books and we do all kinds of other different things.

Liz said, "I like working with my buddies." Mariam said, "I like doing activities with my buddy." Mehdi said, "I like good planning because we have fun." Saad K., Yassine, Ghita, Coral, Karima and Hamza said, "I like the activities we do." Perle said, "I like teaching the buddies." Mohamed said, "I like buddies because it is funny." Mustapha said, "I like organizing for buddies." Hicham said, "I like planning for buddies and when I grow up I will know what to do with my children." Hachem said, "I like planning for buddies, teaching small kids and being patient." Anouk said, "I like small kids and I like taking care of them."

We do buddies in Ms. Melanie's classroom because that is where the buddies are. We do buddies because we need to learn how to take care of small kids. We do buddies on Thursdays before lunch.

By Anouk

◆ REFERENCES

Atwell, N. (1987). *In the middle: Writing, reading and learning with adolescents.* Portsmouth, NH: Boynton/Cook Heinemann.

Bromley, K. (1995). Buddy journals for ESL and native-English-speaking students. *TESOL Journal, 4/3,* 7–11.

Calkins, L. (1994). *The art of teaching writing, 2/e.* Portsmouth, NH: Heinemann.

Cohen, P., Kulik, J., & Kulik, C. (1982). Educational outcomes of tutoring: A meta-analysis of findings. *American Educational Research Journal, 19,* 237–248.

Commission on Standards for School Mathematics. (1989). *Curriculum and evaluation standards for school mathematics.* Reston, VA: National Council of Teachers of Mathematics.

Cook, B., and Urzua, C. (1993, Spring). *The literacy club: A cross-age tutoring/paired reading project.* NCBE (National Clearinghouse for Bilingual Education) Program Information Guide Series: Number 13.

Graves, D. H. (1983). *Writing: Teachers and children at work.* Portsmouth, NH: Heinemann.

Heath, S. B., & Mangiola, L. (1991). *Children of promise: Literate activity in linguistically and culturally diverse classrooms.* Washington, DC: National Education Association.

Juel, C. (1991). Cross-age tutoring between student athletes and at-risk children. *The Reading Teacher, 45,* 178–186.

Labbo, L., & Teale, W. (1990). Cross-age reading: A strategy for helping poor readers. *The Reading Teacher, 43,* 362–369.

Leland, C., & Fitzpatrick, R. (1993). Cross-age interaction builds enthusiasm for reading and writing. *The Reading Teacher, 43,* 292–301.

Peyton, J. K., & Reed, L. (1990). *Dialogue journal writing with nonnative English speakers: A handbook for teachers.* Alexandria, VA: Teachers of English to Speakers of Other Languages.

Rekrut, M. D. (1994). Peer and cross-age tutoring: The lessons of research. *The Journal of Reading, 37/5*, 356–362.

Samway, K. D., Whang, G., & Pippitt, M. (1995). *Buddy reading: Cross-age tutoring in a multicultural school.* Portsmouth, NH: Heinemann.

Wollman–Bonilla, J. (1991). *Response journals.* New York: Scholastic.

◆ RELATED REFERENCES: FOR FURTHER READING

Enright, S. (1991). Supporting children's language development in grade-level and language classrooms. In M. Celce–Murcia (Ed.), *Teaching English as a second or foreign language,* 2/e (pp. 386–402). Boston: Heinle & Heinle.

Graves, D. H., & Hansen, J. (1983). The author's chair. *Language Arts, 60*(2), 176–183.

Green, J., & Meyer, L. (1991). The embeddedness of reading in classroom life: Reading as a situated process. In C. Baker & A. Luke (Eds.), *Toward a critical sociology of reading and pedagogy* (pp. 141–160). Philadelphia: John Benjamins.

Harste, J. C., & Short, K. G., with Burke, C. L. (1988). *Creating classrooms for authors: The reading–writing connection.* Portsmouth, NH: Heinemann.

Teale, W. H. (1982). Toward a theory of how children learn to read and write naturally. *Language Arts, 59*, 555–570.

Wells, G. (1981). *Learning through interaction.* London: Cambridge UP.

◆ THOUGHT STARTERS
for reflection, journal writing, and/or discussion:

1. How does cross-age tutoring facilitate language and literacy acquisition? What do the tutors gain? What do the tutees gain?

2. If you wanted to implement a buddy program, what challenges would you face? What more would you need to know? What kind of modeling would you provide?

3. Discuss the use of buddy journals and their role in literacy and language development. How do they work? Share knowledge of related research.

4. Why do we seem to learn more when we teach others? What do tutors need to consider? Explore implications for the classroom.

◆ PROJECT STARTERS
for writing and research:

1. "Buddy up" with someone who has done reseach in an area that interests you. Several brief sessions may do it. Keep a learning log, and then write up your experience. What did you gain? What did the tutor gain? (Ask him/her.)

2. Review three to four journal articles on cross-age tutoring. Report on uses, variations, problems, and successes of cross-age programs.

3. Ann's work on cross-age tutoring was useful to her own learning. Sketch out the plans for an innovation you would like to implement. How might it change you/your teaching? Check the literature for useful resources. Include a bibliography.

4. Explore the idea of *conversation partners* or *writing partners* for (young) adults in language and/or writing classes. Interview a teacher with related experience and survey the literature for relevant information. Write up your findings.

Afterword: A Look Back at Ethnographic Research

> To those who have read the . . . preceding chapters, the data and findings of this study may well appear self-evident. It may seem that all I had to do was spend enough time . . . to learn—inevitably and unavoid-ably—what I finally learned. In fact, that may seem to be the nature of any ethnographic study when encoun-tered in its final published form. Yet that is not the reality of ethnography as I experienced it . . .
>
> —Andrea Fishman,
> *Amish Literacy*

As I complete this ethnographic study, it is almost three years since I arrived in Morocco on the day I describe in Chapter One, and I am both exhausted and exhilarated by the experience of it all—and by the process of ethnographic writing. I worry that my writing is misleading, making the study there seem too simple, too pat, and my findings self-evident. Conversely, I worry that others will come away from this final published form without a sense that I do indeed have findings. Worry that my attempts to *put the reader there* and to show rather than tell will leave others wondering *What's the point?*

To those interested in ethnographic research, I urge you to read others' work and learn from it. A word of caution though. The finished findings may give the impression that everything will become apparent if you spend enough time in the context you've chosen and just look hard enough in the right direction. Be prepared to feel—for days on end—that you don't know what you are looking at, and you don't always even know where to look. As Andrea Fishman says, the final drafting of others' ethnographic research "starts with closure and works backwards, but ethnography does not" (p. 206).

Such complexity and uncertainty are in the nature of naturalistic research. But knowing that is different from experiencing it. I may appear to know what I am doing and seeing in this published form, but often I did not. Some of my thoughts and conclusions did not become apparent to me, in fact, until the final redrafting of this book. Some of what I hope I've made visible to readers remained invisible to me until almost the very end.

Yet, is it made visible enough? By choosing to share my sense-making through illustrative episodes rather than through more explicit analysis, my plan, however risky, is to make it accessible to readers as input to their own sense-making of related experiences, both lived and learned through others. For my own learning, the potential for generating insight through reflection on related experiences is ethnography's prime value.

Glossary of Foreign Words

Aid el Kabir: an important Islamic feast day, which comes a month after the end of Ramadan and coincides with the closing days of the Muslims' pilgrimage to Mecca

baraka(t): Arabic for *grace,* or *good fortune,* bestowed by Allah upon all believers

bidonville: French pejorative term for *slum.* I have used it here to capture the utter awfulness for the people who live under these conditions.

burnous: a thick, heavy, camel's hair cloak, with a cowl, worn by Moroccan men

caftan: a full-length tunic, with a cowl, traditionally worn by Moroccan women

chai naa-naa: Arabic for *mint tea*

couscous: Moroccan national dish, made of steamed semolina wheat and garnished with meat (lamb, beef, chicken, or fish) and vegetables. Moroccan couscous is often also served with raisins and nuts.

derija: Moroccan term for the dialect of Arabic spoken in Morocco

djellaba: a typical long-sleeved, ankle-length, loose Moroccan garment

Fatima: the name of a daughter of the Prophet Muhammad; the hand of Fatima, as a blessed symbol, is worn as jewelry, woven into carpets, painted on ceramics, and is even drawn on the bumpers of trucks as protection from evil and misfortune.

fondouk: Arabic for *hotel, inn*

habbous: Arabic for a special district surrounding a royal palace. As the district's royal patron, the king designates himself as the protector of the area.

hammam: Arabic for *public bath,* a vital social center in every town and traditional neighborhood in Morocco. Men's and women's *hammams* are usually separate facilities. Women take their children, and spend time socializing with other women while they bathe and relax.

henna: a reddish powder ground from the leaves of the henna plant, used by Moroccan women as a cosmetic dye for coloring hair, and for decorating feet and palms for ritual ceremonies

ksar: (*ksour,* pl.) a fortified Berber village, found throughout valleys in the south of Morocco, formed of massive walls built from mud–clay pisé of the riverbanks, often monumental in design and decorated with bold, geometric patterns incised or painted on (Ellingham & McVeigh, 1985, p. 253)

lycée: French for *secondary school;* in the French educational system, *lycée* schooling leads to a baccalaureate degree, a degree higher than the U.S. high school diploma.

Maghrib: Arabic for *west,* i.e, the western part of the Islamic world, which is North Africa; in Moroccan Arabic, the word means *Morocco*

marhabebik: Arabic for *welcome* (to you: *-ik*)

medina(t): Arabic for *city;* in post-colonial North Africa, the word connotes the Arab *quarter,* that is, the old city.

quartier: French for *quarter,* i.e., a neighborhood or district of a city

souk: Arabic for *marketplace* in the old city, with narrow passageways and stalls or small shops

tagine: Moroccan stew, usually cooked in a clay pot; lamb, beef, chicken, or fish, cooked with potatoes, peas, and peppers, in a tomato sauce

tamazight: Berber word designating one of the several Berber dialects of North Africa

tchoutchouka: a mixed salad of chopped tomatoes and peppers, common across North Africa

thé à la menthe: French for *mint tea*

References

Ardizzone, T. (1992). *Larabi's ox: Stories of Morocco*. Minneapolis: Milkweed Editions.

Atwell, N. (1987). *In the middle: Writing, reading and learning with adolescents*. Portsmouth, NH: Boynton/Cook Heinemann.

Atwell, N. (1991). *Side by side*. Portsmouth, NH: Heinemann.

Au, K. H. (1993). *Literacy instruction in multicultural settings*. Orlando, FL: Harcourt Brace Jovanovich.

Bissex, G. L. (1980). *GNYS AT WRK: A child learns to read and write*. Cambridge, MA: Harvard UP.

Blazer, B. (1986). I want to talk to you about writing: Five year olds speak. In B. Schiefflin & P. Gilmore (Eds.), *The acquisition of literacy: Ethnographic perspectives, Vol. XXI: Advances in discourse processes* (pp. 75–109). Norwood, NJ: Ablex.

Bowles, P. (1993). The baptism of solitude. In *Too far from home: The selected writings of Paul Bowles*. Hopewell, NJ: Ecco Press.

Britton, J. (1989). Writing-and-reading in the classroom. In A. H. Dyson (Ed.), *Collaboration through writing and reading: Exploring possibilities* (pp. 217–246). Urbana, IL: National Council of Teachers of English.

Bromley, K. (1995). Buddy journals for ESL and native-English-speaking students. *TESOL Journal, 4/3*, 7–11.

Bruner, J. V. (1985). Vygotsky: A historical and conceptual perspective. In J. V. Wertsch (Ed.), *Culture, communication, and cognition: Vygotskian perspectives* (pp. 21–34). Cambridge, England: Cambridge UP.

Calkins, L. C. (1994). *The art of teaching writing, 2/e*. Portsmouth, NH: Heinemann.

Canetti, Elias. (1978). *The voices of Marrakesh: A record of a visit*. New York: Farrar Straus Giroux.

Cazden, C. B. (1982). Adult assistance to language development: Scaffolds, models and direct instruction. In R. Parker & F. Davis (Eds.), *Developing literacy: Young children's use of language* (pp. 3–18). Newark, DE: International Reading Association.

Chiseri–Strater, E. (1991). *Academic literacies: The public and private discourse of university students*. Portsmouth, NH: Boynton/Cook Heinemann.

Clay, M. M. (1966). *Emergent reading behaviour*. Unpublished doctoral dissertation, University of Auckland, New Zealand.

Clifford, J. (1983). On ethnographic authority. *Representations 1*: 118–146.

Cohen, P., Kulik, J., & Kulik, C. (1982). Educational outcomes of tutoring: A meta-analysis of findings. *American Educational Research Journal, 19*, 237–248.

Collier, V. (1987). Age and rate of acquisition of second language for academic purposes. *TESOL Quarterly, 21*, 617–641.

Collier, V. (1992). A synthesis of studies examining long-term language-minority student data on academic achievement. *Bilingual Research Journal 16*(1 & 2), 187–212.

Commission on Standards for School Mathematics. (1989). *Curriculum and evaluation standards for school mathematics*. Reston, VA: National Council of Teachers of Mathematics.

Cook, B., & Urzua, C. (1993, Spring). *The literacy club: A cross-age tutoring/paired reading project*. NCBE (National Clearinghouse for Bilingual Education) Program Information Guide Series: Number 13.

Cook–Gumperz, J. (1975). The child as practical reasoner. In M. Sanches & B. C. Blout (Eds.), *Socio-cultural dimensions of language use* (pp. 137–162). New York: Academic Press.

Cummins, J. (1984). *Bilingualism and special education: Issues in assessment and pedagogy*. Clevedon, England: Multilingual Matters.

Dyson, A. H. (1981). *A case study examination of the role of oral language in writing processes of kindergarteners*. Unpublished doctoral dissertation, The University of Texas at Austin.

Dyson, A. H. (1983). The role of oral language in early writing processes. *Research in the Teaching of English, 17*, 1–30.

Dyson, A. H. (1984). Emerging alphabetic literacy in school contexts: Toward defining the gap between school curriculum and child mind. *Written Communication, 1*, 5–55.

Dyson, A. H. (1986). Staying free to dance with the children: The dangers of sanctifying activities in the language arts curriculum. *English Education, 18*, 135–146.

Dyson, A. H. (Ed.). (1989a). *Collaboration through writing and reading: Exploring possibilities*. Urbana, IL: National Council of Teachers of English.

Dyson, A. H. (1989b). *Multiple worlds of childhood writers: Friends learning to write*. New York: Teachers College Press.

Dyson, A. H. (1990). Research currents: Diversity, social responsibility, and the story of literacy development. *Language Arts, 67/2*, 192–205.

Dyson, A. H. (1993). *Social worlds of children learning to write in an urban primary school*. New York: Teachers College Press.

Early, M. (1990). Enabling first and second language learners in the classroom. *Language Arts, 67*, 567–575.

Early, M., Mohan, B., & Hooper, H. (1989). The Vancouver school board language and content project. In J. H. Esling (Ed.), *Multicultural education and policy: ESL in the 1990s* (pp. 107–124). Toronto, Canada: O.I.S.E. Press.

Ellingham, M., & McVeigh, S. (1985). *The rough guide to Morocco.* London and New York: Routledge & Kegan Paul.

Enright, S. (1991). Supporting children's language development in grade-level and language classrooms. In M. Celce–Murcia (Ed.), *Teaching English as a second or foreign language* (pp. 386–402). Boston: Heinle & Heinle.

Ferreiro, E. (1991). Literacy acquisition and the representation of language. In C. Kamii, M. Manning, & G. Manning (Eds.), *Early literacy: A constructivist foundation for whole language* (pp. 31–55). Washington, DC: National Education Association.

Ferreiro, E., & Teberosky, A. (1982). *Literacy before schooling.* Portsmouth, NH: Heinemann.

Fishman, A. (1988). *Amish literacy: What and how it means.* Portsmouth, NH: Heinemann.

Freeman, D. E., & Freeman, Y. S. (1994). *Between worlds: Access to second language acquisition.* Portsmouth, NH: Heinemann.

Freeman, Y. S., & Freeman, D. E. (1992). *Whole language for second language learners.* Portsmouth, NH: Heinemann.

Geertz, C. (1988). *Works and lives: the anthropologist as author.* Stanford: Stanford University Press.

Goodman, Y. (1989). Roots of the whole-language movement. *The Elementary School Journal, 90,* 114–127.

Goodman, Y. (Ed.). (1990). *How children construct literacy.* Newark, DE: International Reading Association.

Graves, D. H. (1983). *Writing: Teachers and children at work.* Portsmouth, NH: Heinemann.

Graves, D. H., & Hansen, J. (1983). The author's chair. *Language Arts, 60*(2), 176–183.

Green, J., & Meyer, L. (1991). The embeddedness of reading in classroom life: Reading as a situated process. In C. Baker & A. Luke (Eds.), *Toward a critical sociology of reading and pedagogy* (pp. 141–160). Philadelphia: John Benjamins.

Hammersley, M. (1990). *Reading ethnographic research: A critical guide.* London: Longman.

Harste, J. C., & Short, K. G., with Burke, C. L. (1988). *Creating classrooms for authors: The reading–writing connection.* Portsmouth, NH: Heinemann.

Harste, J. C., Woodward, V., & Burke, C. L. (1984). *Language stories and literacy lessons.* Portsmouth, NH: Heinemann.

Harste, J. C., Woodward, V., & Burke, C. L. (1991). Examining instructional assumptions. In B. M. Power & R. Hubbard (Eds.), *Literacy in process* (pp. 51–66). Portsmouth, NH: Heinemann.

Heath, S. B. (1980, Winter). The functions and uses of literacy. *Journal of Communication, 30,* 123–133.

Heath, S. B. (1982). Ethnography in education: Defining the essentials. In P. Gilmore & A. A. Glatthorn (Eds.), *Children in and out of school: Ethnography and education* (pp. 33–55). Washington, DC: Center for Applied Linguistics.

Heath, S. B. (1983). *Ways with words: Language, life, and work in communities and classrooms.* New York: Cambridge UP.

Heath, S. B. (1986). Critical factors in literacy development. In S. deCastell, A. Luke, & K. Egan (Eds.), *Literacy, society, and schooling: A reader* (pp. 209-229). New York: Cambridge UP.

Heath, S. B. (1991). A lot of talk about nothing. In B. M. Power & R. Hubbard (Eds.), *Literacy in process* (pp. 79–87). Portsmouth, NH: Heinemann.

Heath, S. B., & Mangiola, L. (1991). *Children of promise: Literate activity in linguistically and culturally diverse classrooms.* Washington, DC: National Education Association.

Hornberger, N. H. (1994). Ethnography. In A. Cumming (Ed.), Alternatives in TESOL research: Descriptive, interpretive, and ideological orientations (pp. 688–690). *TESOL Quarterly, 28*(4), 673–703.

Hudelson, S. (1986). ESL children writing: What we've learned, what we're learning. In P. Rigg & D. S. Enright (Eds.), *Children and ESL: Integrating perspectives* (pp. 25–54). Washington, DC: Teachers of English to Speakers of Other Languages.

Hudelson, S. (1989a). "Teaching" English through content-area activities. In P. Rigg & V. G. Allen (Eds.), *When they don't all speak English: Integrating the ESL student into the regular classroom* (pp. 139–151). Urbana, IL: National Council of Teachers of English.

Hudelson, S. (1989b). *Write on: Children's writing in ESL.* Englewood Cliffs, NJ: Prentice-Hall Regents.

Huss, R. L. (1995). Young children becoming literate in English as a second language. *TESOL Quarterly, 29*(4), 767–774.

Hymes, D. (1974). *Foundations of sociolinguistics: An ethnographic approach.* Philadelphia: University of Pennsylvania Press.

Juel, C. (1991). Cross-age tutoring between student athletes and at-risk children. *The Reading Teacher, 45,* 178–186.

Krashen, S. (1982). *Principles and practice in second language acquisition.* New York: Pergamon Press.

Labbo, L., & Teale, W. (1990). Cross-age reading: A strategy for helping poor readers. *The Reading Teacher, 43,* 362–369.

Langer, J. A. (1986). *Children reading and writing: Structures and strategies.* Norwood, NJ: Ablex.

Leki, I. (1995). Coping strategies of ESL students in writing tasks across the disciplines. *TESOL Quarterly, 29,* 235–260.

Leland, C., & Fitzpatrick, R. (1993). Cross-age interaction builds enthusiasm for reading and writing. *The Reading Teacher, 43,* 292–301.

Luria, A. R. (1982). *Language and cognition.* New York: Wiley.

Mernissi, F. (1987). *Beyond the veil: Male–female dynamics in modern Muslim society.* Bloomington: Indiana UP.

Moll, L. C. (Ed.). (1990). *Vygotsky and education: Instructional implications and applications of sociohistorical psychology.* Cambridge, MA: Cambridge UP.

Moll, L. C., & Diaz, R. (1987). Teaching writing as communication: The uses of ethnographic findings in classroom practice. In D. Bloome (Ed.), *Literacy and schooling* (pp. 195–221). Norwood, NJ: Ablex.

Nitzkin, A. (1996). The metaphorical roots of writing. Unpublished research paper, English Department, University of New Orleans.

Peyton, J. K., & Reed, L. (1990). *Dialog journal writing with nonnative English speakers: A handbook for teachers.* Alexandria, VA: Teachers of English to Speakers of Other Languages.

Rekrut, M. D. (1994). Peer and cross-age tutoring: The lessons of research. *The Journal of Reading, 37/5,* 356–362.

Rivers, W. J. (1988). *Problems in composition: A Vygotskian perspective.* Unpublished doctoral dissertation, University of Delaware, Newark.

Samway, K. D., Whang, G., & Pippitt, M. (1995). *Buddy reading: Cross-age tutoring in a multicultural school.* Portsmouth, NH: Heinemann.

Scinto, L. E. M. (1986). *Written language and psychological development.* New York: Academic Press.

Spack, R. (1997). The acquisition of academic literacy in a second language: A longitudinal case study. *Written Communication, 14*(1), 3–62.

Steward, E. P. (1995). *Beginning writers in the zone of proximal development.* Hillsdale, NJ: Lawrence Erlbaum.

Sulzby, E. (1985). Kindergartners as writers and readers. In M. Farr (Ed.), *Advances in writing research, volume one: Children's early writing development* (pp. 127–199). Norwood, NJ: Ablex.

Sulzby, E. (1986). Writing and reading: Signs of oral and written language organization in the young child. In W. H. Teale & E. Sulzby (Eds.), *Emergent literacy: Writing and reading* (pp. 50–89). Norwood, NJ: Ablex.

Szwed, J. F. (1981). The ethnography of literacy. In M. F. Whiteman (Ed.), *The nature, development, and teaching of written communication,* Vol. 1 (pp. 13-23). Hillsdale, NJ: Erlbaum.

Teale, W. H. (1982). Toward a theory of how children learn to read and write naturally. *Language Arts, 59,* 555–570.

Teale, W. H., & Sulzby, E. (Eds.). (1986). *Emergent literacy: Writing and reading.* Norwood, NJ: Ablex.

Tharp, R. G., & Gallimore, R. (1988). *Rousing minds to life.* Cambridge, MA: Cambridge UP.

Van Maanen, J. (1988). *Tales of the field: On writing ethnography.* Chicago: University of Chicago Press.

Vygotsky, L. S. (1978). *Mind in society: The development of higher psychological processes.* Cambridge, MA: MIT Press.

Wagner, D. A., Messick, B. M., & Spratt, J. (1986). Studying literacy in Morocco. In B. Schieffelin & P. Gilmore (Eds.), *The acquisition of literacy: Ethnographic perspectives* (pp. 233–260). Norwood, NJ: Ablex.

Watson–Gegeo, K. A. (1988). Ethnography in ESL: Defining the essentials. *TESOL Quarterly, 22*(4), 575–592.

Wells, G. (1981). *Learning through interaction.* London: Cambridge UP.

Wertsch, J. V. (1984). The zone of proximal development: Some conceptual issues. In B. Rogoff & J. V. Wertsch (Eds.), *Children's learning in the "zone of proximal development"* (pp. 3–21). San Francisco, CA: Jossey-Bass.

Wollman–Bonilla, J. (1991). *Response journals.* New York: Scholastic.

Wong Fillmore, L. (1989). Teaching English through content: Instructional reform in programs for language minority students. In J. H. Esling (Ed.), *Multicultural education and policy: ESL in the 1990s (pp. 125–143).* Toronto, Canada: O.I.S.E. Press.

Yule, G. (1996). *The study of language, 2/e.* Cambridge, MA: Cambridge UP.

Index

Note: Page numbers in italic type indicate full citations of authors' works; page numbers followed by n indicate footnotes.